# Organized Crime in America: Concepts and Controversies

# Organized Crime in America: Concepts and Controversies

## Edited by

## Timothy S. Bynum

Issues in Crime and Justice
Volume 1

Sponsored by the
Academy of Criminal Justice Sciences

CRIMINAL JUSTICE PRESS
a division of
Willow Tree Press, Inc.
Monsey, New York
1987

**Library of Congress Cataloging-in-Publication Data**

Organized crime in America.

   (Issues in crime and justice; v. 1)
   Includes bibiliographies.
   1.  Organized crime—United States—History.
2.  Organized crime investigation—United States.
I.  Bynum, Timothy S.  II.  Series: Issues in crime and
justice (Monsey, N.Y.); v. 1.
HV6446.074  1987      364.1'06'073      86-29261
ISBN 0-9606960-2-4

# Table of Contents

# About the Contributors

**Timothy S. Bynum** is an associate professor in the School of Criminal Justice, Michigan State University.

**Howard Abadinsky** is an associate professor in the Program in Criminal Justice, St. Xavier College.

**Jay S. Albanese** is an associate professor in the Department of Political Science and Criminal Justice, Niagara University.

**Alan A. Block** is a professor in the Administration of Justice Program, Pennsylvania State University.

**John Dombrink** is an assistant professor in the Program in Social Ecology, University of California, Irvine.

**Donna Hale** is an assistant professor in the Department of Criminal Justice, University of Baltimore.

**Dennis E. Hoffman** is an associate professor in the Department of Criminal Justice, University of Nebraska at Omaha.

**Peter A. Lupsha** is a professor in the Department of Political Science, University of New Mexico.

**Malorie Melrose** is a law student and a graduate of the University of California, Irvine.

**Merry Morash** is an associate professor in the School of Criminal Justice, Michigan State University.

**Humbert S. Nelli** is a professor in the Department of History, University of Kentucky.

**Frank R. Scarpitti** is a professor in the Department of Sociology, University of Delaware.

**Kip Schlegel** is an assistant professor in the Department of Criminal Justice, University of Nebraska, Lincoln.

# Part I: Introduction

# Controversies in the Study of Organized Crime

## Timothy S. Bynum

No other topic in criminology so fascinates the American public as organized crime. The immense popularity of *The Godfather*, and the frequent, often sensationalized journalistic accounts of organized crime activities, demonstrate the insatiable public appetite for news of the underworld.

Yet, in spite or perhaps because of this public attention, a mythology surrounds organized crime in which stereotypes abound and assumptions go unchallenged. The popular conception equates organized crime with a nationally organized, highly structured Italian-American criminal society known as the Mafia, and it exerts great influence on public policy. But many scholars maintain that preoccupation with this "Mafia mystique" seriously hampers understanding of organized crime. And a growing body of research suggests that organized crime is not an alien conspiracy but is, instead, a "normal" product of American society.

Both the popular and scholarly literatures on organized crime in America abound with controversies spawned by anomalies in the familiar Mafia paradigm of organized crime. To set the stage for the papers in this anthology, the literature on two of the main controversies—relating to the definition of organized crime, and to its structure and activities—will be briefly surveyed.

## THE DEFINITION CONTROVERSY

One of the principal problems in the study of organized crime is the lack of a consistent definition. Perhaps because of the dominance of the popular conception of organized crime, few writers worry about precise definitions. However, greater definitional clarity should be attempted for both legal and scholarly purposes.

How is organized crime to be defined for the purposes of law enforcement and prosecution? When a prosecutor seeks additional sanctions

3

against a defendant because he belongs to an organized crime group, what indicators should be present to substantiate such involvement? The major prosecution tool is the Organized Crime Control Act of 1970, which includes the more commonly known Racketeer Influenced and Corrupt Organizations (RICO) provisions. Paradoxically, even this important piece of crime control legislation only discusses the phenomenon of organized crime in generalities, without reference to specific activities and definitions (Abadinsky, 1981a). Moreover, several years after passage of this legislation, a review of federal efforts to combat organized crime concluded that the definition of organized crime used by the U.S. Justice Department contributed to the ineffectiveness of control programs (U.S. General Accounting Office, 1977).

Not only law enforcement and government commissions, but criminologists too, have been unable to formulate a clear definition of organized crime. Since the findings of many research studies are largely a function of the way research questions were framed, how organized crime is defined may influence the public policy implications of research findings. For example, findings on whether organized crime is distinct from white collar crime hinge largely on how organized crime is defined.

Definitional difficulties were deliberately circumvented by the Task Force on Organized Crime of the U.S. National Advisory Committee on Criminal Justice Standards and Goals, which proclaimed that: "No single definition is believed inclusive enough to meet the needs of the many different individuals and groups throughout the country that may use it as a means to develop an organized crime control effort" (1976:7). However politically feasible such avoidance may be, it should not deter efforts to clarify the definition.

The existing definitional ambiguity does not imply that there has been a lack of attempts to define organized crime. Indeed, many definitions have been put forward: See, for example, Maltz, 1976; U.S. National Advisory Committee, 1976; Blakey, Goldstock, and Rogovin, 1978; Abadinsky, 1981a, and Maltz, 1985. Some definitions have been extremely broad and not particularly helpful in differentiating specific organized crime activities; they have a tautological quality, equivalent to saying "organized crime is crime that is organized." On the other hand, definitions that are quite narrow often result in the exclusion of behaviors that should be included within organized crime. For example, an exclusive identification of organized crime with the Mafia leads researchers to ignore similar activities by other organized groups (e.g., narcotics distribution by Hell's Angels), as well as the linkages between organized crime and legitimate business.

Another central definitional issue is whether organized crime refers to types of criminal behavior or to types of groups or organizations. Although many earlier definitions focused principally on the activities of organized crime, much recent research suggests the importance of relating these activities to the type of group that commits them (Maltz, 1985). Thus, an adequate definition of organized crime must incorporate descriptions of the activities and the group(s), and their interrelationships.

Hagan's (1983) fruitful approach was to review definitions of organized crime that have appeared in books and government reports of the last 15 years in search of common definitional elements. Among thirteen authors there was some consensus that organized crime generally involves a continuing enterprise that rationally operates to make a profit through illicit activities. There was also considerable agreement that organized crime involves the use of violence, or at least the threat of violence, to maintain its operation. In addition, the corruption of public officials was often viewed as a necessary ingredient for the successful operation of organized crime. There was much less agreement, however, on other characteristics of organized crime, including its reported monopoly over services, code of secrecy, and restricted membership.

Michael Maltz (1985) has made further progress with additional analysis of common organized crime characteristics found in the literature. Maltz concluded that organized crime generally requires: some form of public sector corruption to assure its continued operation; the potential for use of violence; continuous operation that promotes group cohesion; and, involvement in multiple enterprises. Though most organized crime groups are involved in legitimate businesses, Maltz indicated that this is not a necessary characteristic. Not all organized crime groups are necessarily structured in accordance with the traditional Mafia paradigm. Similarly, while some organized crime groups are highly sophisticated and disciplined, these characteristics are not typical. Thus, Maltz's profile of organized crime differs dramatically from and challenges the traditional definition of organized crime as being synonymous with the Mafia.

These recent definitional explorations by Hagan and Maltz appear to point the way toward more clarity in defining organized crime, although much ambiguity and lack of consensus still exists.

## Controversies about Structure and Activities

Related to the definitional debates are multiple controversies about the structure and activities of organized crime.

Research about the structure of organized crime often examines the relevance of the dominant paradigm of organized crime as the Mafia.

This image was formed largely from testimony presented before legislative hearings and government commissions. Particularly important was the testimony of Joseph Valachi before the U.S. Senate Subcommittee on Investigations in 1963. Although organized criminal activity and the Mafia had been the subject of earlier commissions and investigations (particularly the Kefauver hearings in 1950), little direct evidence had substantiated the existence of this national criminal conspiracy (Albanese, 1985). For government investigations and many criminologists, Valachi's testimony supplied this missing link of evidence.

Valachi testified that he had been a member of a nationally organized group of Italian-Americans, known as La Cosa Nostra, which existed principally for making profits from illicit activities. This group was highly structured, with each crime "family" having an individual "boss," and other family members having structured roles and responsibilities under him. The use of violence was an important characteristic of the operation, as evidenced in a tumultuous power struggle between Italian-American gangs that had resulted in sixty murders (U.S. Senate, 1963).

Several years later, and based largely on Valachi's testimony, the Task Force on Organized Crime of the President's Commission on Law Enforcement and Criminal Justice reaffirmed the existence of the Mafia (U.S. President's Commission, 1967). Further, as an outgrowth of his activities as a principal consultant to the task force, Donald Cressey (1969) published an influential book, *Theft of the Nation*, which reinforced the view that organized crime is a national criminal conspiracy as described by Valachi.

The description of organized crime that emerged during this period became the dominant influence on public attitudes and government policy. Galliher and Cain (1974), for example, demonstrated its predominance in introductory criminology textbooks.

This dominant view, however, was not without its critics. Valachi's testimony, in particular, was criticized for substantial inconsistencies and other problems (Hawkins, 1969; Smith, 1975; Block, 1978; Nelli, 1981). For example, Albanese (1985) questioned why Valachi's testimony did not lead to subsequent prosecutions, why no one had ever heard of La Cosa Nostra prior to Valachi, and why government officials were unable to verify more than four of the many murders than Valachi recalled.

Even though Valachi's testimony was challenged, government commissions still made it the basis of their findings and policy recommendations. Hawkins (1969) asserted that Valachi's inconsistencies were either overlooked or explained away as unimportant because they fit the government's preconceived view of organized crime. Based on his review of the evidence about the existence of La Cosa Nostra, Hawkins (1969) concluded that acceptance of the Mafia paradigm was based on faith rather than demonstrable evidence.

Other criticisms of the "alien conspiracy" (Smith, 1980) view of organized crime also attacked the dominant Mafia paradigm. In response to government officials' rhetoric about the threat to the American way of life presented by the "alien conspiracy," some scholars have sought to demonstrate that organized crime is a reflection of and natural outgrowth from American society. For example, in an analysis similar to Cloward and Ohlin's (1960) study of subcultural criminal behavior, Bell (1953) argued that organized crime provided a ladder of social mobility for members of a succession of ethnic groups to attain the "good life" in America. Commenting upon the Kefauver hearings, Bell (1953:125) noted:

> But what Senator Kefauver and company failed to understand was that the mobsters, like the gamblers, and the entire gangdom generally, were seeking to become quasi-respectable and establish a place for themselves in American life. For the mobsters, by and large, had immigrant roots, and crime, as the pattern showed, was a route of social ascent and place in American life.

Other critiques of the Mafia paradigm have emphasized the localized structure of organized crime, and its lack of rigid organization. This structure has been characterized as a series of individual "patron-client" relationships principally organized according to the particular criminal activity (Ianni, 1973; Albini, 1971). Thus, criminal groups are "organized" more as social systems reinforced by subcultural values than as the bureaucracies depicted by government commissions (Albanese, 1985). This perspective gains credibility from the fact that similar conclusions were obtained using several different research methodologies: namely, participant observation (Ianni, 1972), interviews with an organized crime informant (Abadinsky, 1981b), and analysis of the federal government's own organized crime files (Anderson, 1979).

Another alternative to the Mafia-centered view of organized crime, also stressing the "normalcy" of this activity, makes use of economic analysis techniques. Increasingly, research is based upon the assumption that organized crime operates on the same market principles that govern legitimate enterprises. Such analysis encourages a recognition of the porous boundaries that separate the business of crime, the crime of business, and legitimate business operations. Thus, Smith (1980) argues that organized crime can be placed on an "enterprise spectrum," with legal activities on one end and criminal ones on the other. The underlying and unifying principle of this spectrum is that all business enterprises are organized for profit; differences between legal and illegal enterprises are matters more of degree than of kind. Smith (1980:370) notes:

> [T]hat enterprise takes place across a spectrum that includes both business and certain kinds of crime; that behavioral theory regarding organizations in general and business in particular can be applied to the entire spectrum; and that while theories about conspiracy and ethnicity have some pertinence to organized crime, they are clearly subordinate to a theory of enterprise.

The adoption of this economic orientation toward organized crime allows for a less ideological view that has greater explanatory power (Albanese, 1982). Although associated with recent research, this approach may be traced back to Robert Merton, who over forty years ago noted that organized crime and political corruption were not economically distinguishable from legitimate business (Merton, 1957).

A recent study of organized crime involvement in the bookmaking and numbers operations in New York City (Reuter and Rubinstein, 1978) further illustrates the utility of the economic perspective. These illegal gambling activities were not highly organized, not centrally controlled, not exclusively the province of one organization, and not highly disciplined or violent. Reuter and Rubinstein (1978:63–64) explain that:

> It is not our intention to deny the existence of a Mafia. In this respect we differ from earlier critics . . . Our own research does show that there is a Mafia, and probably more than one, although it is far less distinctive than is normally alleged and its relation to other criminal groups is not clearly defined. . . . The Mafia is clearly only a part of the world of stable, hierarchical criminal organizations.

While there continues to be disagreement among researchers regarding the structure and definition controversies, there does appear to be an emerging consensus regarding the diversity of organized criminal behavior (Reuter and Rubinstein, 1978). In recognition of the necessity of a more inclusive approach, and to overcome the traditional connotations of the term "organized crime," some authors have encouraged replacement of that term by the concept of "illicit enterprise" (Smith, 1980) or "organizational crime" (Albanese, 1985).

## ADDRESSING THE CONTROVERSIES: THE SELECTIONS IN THIS VOLUME

The selections of original research prepared for this volume reflect the current diversity of research on organized crime. Some authors directly investigate the adequacy of traditional assumptions about organized crime (see, for example, the chapters by Abadinsky and Schlegel), while others examine the breadth of organized crime activities and the inter-relationship between society and organized crime (see, for example, the chapter by Albanese).

The initial section is devoted to traditional, illicit organized crime activities, and addresses some of the familiar assumptions about organized crime. Humbert Nelli has provided a history of American "syndicate crime" in the twentieth century, documenting the rise of the Italian criminal syndicate. He notes the waning influence of this group as other organized criminal syndicates gained power. Similarly, Peter Lupsha documents both the historical and contemporary activities of the Italian criminal syndicate in narcotics trafficking, an activity supposedly shunned by the top leadership of the organization.

The next two selections investigate two other aspects of the traditional view of organized crime. Howard Abadinsky challenges the stereotypic view of the Mafia as being a highly structured bureaucratic organization, instead analogizing it to a franchising operation. And Kip Schlegel, based on analysis of the De Cavalcante and De Carlo wiretap transcripts, concludes—as have Ianni (1972) and Anderson (1979)—that organized crime activities are not as violent as the Mafia paradigm suggests.

The final section explores non-traditional aspects of organized crime, especially its involvement in legitimate business and government affairs. Jay Albanese identifies factors that make a market "ripe" for organized crime involvement.

The final two chapters describe organized criminal activities in specific legitimate markets and relate it to government corruption. The research by Frank Scarpitti and Alan Block exposes organized criminal involvement in the toxic waste disposal industry and the corruption that allows it to flourish. Merry Morash and Donna Hale explore how public perceptions of government corruption were influenced by media presentations about organized crime involvement in the trucking industry and its regulatory agency, the Interstate Commerce Commission.

## CONCLUSION

Individually and collectively, the studies in this volume contribute significantly to the study of American organized crime, helping to extend
and refine alternative perspectives to the simplistic Mafia paradigm. The
nine chapters that follow again demonstrate convincingly that organized
crime is too diverse to fit usefully into a single, static Mafia model. This
diversity is documented and explained through the use of several research
perspectives that deserve further exploration, including: organized
crime's historical development and changes over time; the varying structures of syndicate groups and their relation to principal business activities; conditions in the markets of legal enterprises that facilitate or impede
infiltration by illicit organizations; the varying effectiveness of public
and private sector strategies to contain organized crime; and, the shaping
and impact of public perceptions about organized crime influence in the
economic and political arenas.

## References

Abadinsky, Howard (1981a). *Organized Crime*. Boston: Allyn and Bacon.
_____ (1981b). *The Mafia in America: An Oral History*. New York:
        Praeger.
Albanese, Jay (1982). "What Lockheed and La Cosa Nostra Have in Com-
        mon: The Effect of Ideology on Criminal Justice Policy." *Crime &
        Delinquency* 28 (April): 211–232.
_____ (1985). *Organized Crime in America*. Cincinnati, OH: Anderson.
Albini, Joseph (1971). *The American Mafia: Genesis of a Legend*. New
        York: Irvington.
Anderson, Annelise (1979). *The Business of Organized Crime*. Stanford,
        CA: Hoover Institution Press.
Bell, Daniel (1953). "Crime as an American Way of Life." *Antioch Review*
        13 (June):131–154.
Blakey, Robert, Ronald Goldstock and Charles Rogovin (1978). *Rackets
        Bureaus: Investigation and Prosecution of Organized Crime*.
        Washington, DC: U.S. National Institute of Law Enforcement and
        Criminal Justice.
Block, Alan (1978). "History and the Study of Organized Crime." *Urban
        Life* 6:455–474.
Cloward, Richard and Lloyd Ohlin (1960). *Delinquency and Oppor-
        tunity*. New York: Free Press.

Cressey, Donald (1969). *Theft of the Nation.* New York: Harper and Row.

Galliher, John and James Cain (1974). "Citation Support for the Mafia Myth in Criminology Textbooks." *American Sociologist* 9 (May):68–74.

Hagan, Frank (1983). "The Organized Crime Continuum: A Further Specification of a New Conceptual Model." *Criminal Justice Review* 8 (Spring):52–57.

Hawkins, Gordon (1969). "God and the Mafia." *Public Interest* 14:24–51.

Ianni, Francis (1972). *A Family Business: Kinship and Social Control in Organized Crime.* New York: Russell Sage.

———— (1973). *Ethnic Succession in Organized Crime. Washington, DC:* U.S. Government Printing Office.

Maltz, Michael (1976). "On Defining Organized Crime." *Crime & Delinquency* 22 (July):338–346.

———— (1985). "Toward Defining Organized Crime." In: *The Politics and Economics of Organized Crime*, edited by Herbert Alexander and Gerald Caiden. Lexington, MA: Lexington Books. Pp. 21–35.

Merton, Robert (1957). *Social Theory and Social Structure.* New York: Free Press.

Nelli, Humbert (1981). *The Business of Crime: Italians and Syndicate Crime in the United States.* Chicago: University of Chicago Press.

Reuter, Peter and Jonathan Rubinstein (1978). "Fact, Fancy, and Organized Crime." *Public Interest* 53 (Fall):45–67.

Smith, Dwight (1975). *The Mafia Mystique.* New York: Basic Books.

———— (1980). "Paragons, Pariahs, and Pirates: A Spectrum Based Theory of Enterprise." *Crime & Delinquency* 26 (July):358–386.

U.S. General Accounting Office (1977). *War on Organized Crime Faltering—Federal Strike Forces Not Getting Job Done.* Report GGD-77 17. Washington, DC: U.S. General Accounting Office.

U.S. National Advisory Committee on Criminal Justice Standards and Goals (1976). *Organized Crime: Report of the Task Force on Organized Crime.* Washington, DC: U.S. Government Printing Office.

U.S. President's Commission on Law Enforcement and Criminal Justice (1967). *Task Force Report: Organized Crime.* Washington, DC: U.S. Government Printing Office.

U.S. Senate Committee on Government Operations, Permanent Subcommittee on Investigations (1963). *Organized Crime and Illicit Traffic in Narcotics: Hearings Part I.* 88th Congress, First Session. Washington, DC: U.S. Government Printing Office.

# Part II:
# History and
# Traditional Activities
# of Organized Crime

# A Brief History of American Syndicate Crime

## Humbert S. Nelli

*U.S. criminal syndicates first appeared in the 1860s and '70s as gambling interests in New York, Chicago, and other cities organized to fight reform elements. Although Prohibition did not cause syndicate crime, it was a powerful impetus in its growth. Repeal, therefore, did not have the desired and expected effect of destroying the nascent organizations. Instead of disappearing, syndicates thrived in a wide range of other enterprises, including gambling, which had been the cornerstone of the original syndicates. Since World War II, syndicates have enjoyed a golden age. They have reaped millions of dollars from established money-makers like gambling, racketeering, and loansharking, and millions more from developing new fields of entrepreneurial crime like stolen securities. Despite internal and external tensions, crime syndicates historically have been flexible enough to survive by satisfying newly perceived needs as well as the more traditional vices. Therefore, it seems likely that the business of crime will continue to prosper in the foreseeable future.*

Even before Prohibition gave a powerful impetus to American syndicate crime, Chicago Crime Commission Operating Director Henry Barrett Chamberlain could observe that "modern crime, like modern business, is tending toward centralization, organization, and commercialization. Ours is a business nation. Our criminals apply business methods. . . . The men and women of evil have formed trusts" (Chicago Crime Commission, 1919). Businesses offering illegal commodities cater to the needs or interests of a segment of the general public, which in turn views the syndicates as providers of desired services and commodities. This has made it possible for criminal syndicates to obtain protection from politicians, police and, on occasion, even the courts—protection that has enabled the syndicates to continue operating in cities across the nation.

15

Criminal syndicates are illicit business organizations established to further underworld interests in such economic endeavors as bootlegging, gambling, loansharking, narcotics, and business and labor racketeering. The term generally employed to describe these enterprises, "organized crime," has been used in so many different contexts and to describe such a wide variety of illegal activities (from relatively unstructured to highly centralized) that it no longer has a precise meaning. Therefore, this study uses the term "syndicate crime" to refer to illegal business enterprises.

The origins of syndicate crime in America can be traced back to the 1860s and '70s, when gambling syndicates were formed in New York, Chicago, New Orleans, and other cities to counter a threat posed by the emergence of political reform groups. For example, in 1867 the Anti-Gambling Society of New York staged successful raids on several of the city's major gambling houses, and John "Old Smoke" Morrissey led the counterattack of the gambling forces. The city's gamblers contributed money, which Morrissey doled out both to reformers and police, with the result that "for some years there were no further raids" (Chafetz, 1960: 290–91). By 1870, Morrissey and his fellow gamblers had emerged as a major force in New York City machine politics.

In 1870, a formal gambling system also existed in New Orleans, whereby the gambling interests pooled their resources to meet the monetary demands of police officers, from commissioners down to patrolmen. Thus, the *New Orleans Times* reported on June 9, 1870 that "this is the day set aside every month by the Metropolitan Board of Police for collection of its $1,400 blackmail, in return for which it grants immunity and support to gamblers." The spirit of cooperation apparently extended to politicians too, which the paper ruefully pointed out: "As not the least notice has been taken of the exposé made recently, it is now taken for granted that both the State and city administrations endorse the outrage as regular."

A similar system evolved at about the same time in Chicago. In the aftermath of the Great Fire, reform forces organized under the leadership of Mayor Joseph Medill to drive the criminal elements from the city. The gamblers responded in the next election by successfully supporting a mayoral candidate sympathetic to their interests. In the following years a pattern emerged in which a strong criminal organization exerted great influence over politicians, political processes, and the police (Peterson, 1952; Landesco, 1968).

Gambling was the original impetus for the formation of criminal syndicates and remained the principal source of income for the organizations during the half century preceding Prohibition. The operations of the early criminal syndicates were carefully coordinated with, and often even controlled by, local machine politicians and police. An example is New York City where, in the years prior to Prohibition, a three-man board composed of a Tammany Hall representative, a police department official, and a spokesman for the city's gambling interests presided over syndicate activities (Abadinsky, 1983).

## THE NOBLE EXPERIMENT

When the Eighteenth Amendment and the Prohibition Enforcement Act (or Volstead Act) went into effect on January 16, 1920, the American public and its elected officials had no conception of the violence, corruption, and disrespect for the law that the so-called "Noble Experiment" would cause or encourage. In fact, Prohibition was ushered in with a great deal of optimism and hope. In a statement released to the press on the eve of Prohibition, the Anti-Saloon League of New York observed that "at one minute past midnight tomorrow a new nation will be born." It then went on to predict that "tonight John Barleycorn makes his last will and testament. Now for an era of clean thinking and clean living!" (*New York Herald*, January 15, 1920.)

This optimistic outlook died almost immediately. Within hours after John Barleycorn was supposedly put to rest, Volstead Act violations were reported in various cities, large and small, across the nation. Within days, police departments were carrying out raids in an effort to end the growing, and highly profitable, traffic in illicit alcohol. "Dry" laws or not, Americans wanted their drinks, and were ready to do business with anyone who could supply them.

The early 1920s comprised a period of intense competition among criminal entrepreneurs attracted by Prohibition's economic opportunities. The small capital outlay required to enter the business, and the potential for high financial returns, convinced formerly law-abiding citizens as well as small-time criminals to try their luck in a highly competitive but—at least in the early years after the passage of the Volstead Act —a wide-open field of enterprise (Sullivan, 1930).

Bootlegging was especially attractive to already existing criminal syndicates. The network of contacts with police, politicians, and members of the legal system developed during decades of illegal gambling activities, prostitution, and labor racketeering, were readily adapted to the new situation. Violation of the liquor laws was more acceptable to the public than the other forms of criminal enterprise. Even the murder and maiming of rival gang members in the scramble to expand markets and increase profits stirred remarkably little anger or dismay. To many Americans, such situations resembled the old Wild West shoot-outs. Only when innocent bystanders, and especially children, were injured or killed did public opinion demand action against the gangsters. The underworld apparently sensed the importance of public relations and the need to limit violence to insiders. Those who violated the rule to "only kill each other" were dealt with severely (Thompson and Raymond, 1940).

The bootlegging business was a violent and vicious line of economic activity. Markets were expanded, mergers formed, or partnerships ended either at the point of a gun or with the implied threat of violence. Competitors as well as unwanted or unneeded associates were eliminated in a direct and permanent manner. The method usually employed was, of course, the "one-way ride." Literally hundreds of criminals were murdered in Chicago, New York, and other cities as fierce gangland wars were fought over the vast profits to be obtained from the illicit sale of alcoholic beverages (Burns, 1931).

## COOPERATION AND CONSOLIDATION

Although intense competition existed and a great deal of blood was shed, the general tendency during the "Lawless Era" was toward cooperation, and consolidation. In the early days of Prohibition, there existed an open market situation with unrestrained competition and uncertainty of supply and distribution. While shootings, murder, and hijackings generally did not provoke public outrage or force effective action on the part of police or courts, criminals came to realize that such behavior was undesirable from a pragmatic business standpoint. The reason, very simply, was the element of uncertainty injected into operations. As a result, although considerable violence continued to characterize bootlegging, certain individuals or groups emerged as dominant forces by the end of Prohibition.

From New York to Kansas City, and from Chicago to San Francisco, these men established their ascendancy because they encouraged, or even demanded, cooperation rather than competition. Although Italians were to be found in criminal syndicates in all the major cities across the United States, they did not constitute the only criminal force during Prohibition. The so-called Capone syndicate, which had established its hegemony over Chicago's gangland by the beginning of the 1930s, contained large numbers of Italians, but was not limited in membership to any one ethnic group. Among the non-Italians in the organization's hierarchy were Jack Guzik, who was widely regarded as the "brains" of the gang, Murray "the Camel" Humphries, Sam "Golf Bag" Hunt, Dennis "Duke" Cooney, Hymie Levin, and Edward Vogel (Chicago Crime Commission, 1920s, 1930s).

Syndicate crime in Boston was headed by Jewish mobsters: first by Charles "King" Solomon and, after his murder in 1933, by Hyman Abrams. In Philadelphia during the late 1920s, the most powerful bootlegging gang was bossed by a Jewish former prize-fight promoter named Max "Boo Boo" Hoff. Other syndicates, composed of Italians, Poles, Irish, and other ethnics also operated in the "City of Brotherly Love" during this period. Jewish criminals, led by Moe Dalitz, Sam Tucker, Morris Kleinman, and Louis Rathkopf, made a fortune importing liquor from Canada across Lake Erie by boat and plane to their home base of Cleveland. From Cleveland they distributed high-quality Canadian liquor throughout Ohio and Pennsylvania, and even New York (U.S. Internal Revenue Service, 1920s, 1930s; Messick, 1967).

Jewish criminals in Detroit, the so-called Purple Gang, prospered for several years as suppliers of Canadian whiskey for the Capone organization in Chicago. By 1931, however, the Purple Gang as well as other bootlegging groups in Detroit had been elbowed aside by Joseph Zerilli, Pete Licavoli, Angelo Meli and other Italian gangsters. Italians also played a prominent role in booze wars carried on in the 1920s in Kansas City, Denver, and Los Angeles, and emerged in a dominant position in those cities by the end of the decade. In contrast, no individual or group was able to win undisputed control in either New Orleans or San Francisco. In the Louisiana metropolis, state and local politicians maintained a tight rein over the local groups, while in San Francisco police officers determined which illegal activities would be permitted as well as which criminals would be allowed to operate. Thus a grand jury report released on March 16, 1937, and printed in the *San Francisco News*, disclosed that each of San Francisco's four police captains had for years controlled gambling, prostitution, and other illegal activities in his own district (U.S. Senate *Hearings*, 1951; Engelmann, 1971).

The situation was far more vicious and complex in New York than in any other American city. With its numerous gangs and an enormous population offering the richest market for illicit alcohol, New York during the 1920s featured a bewildering maze of shifting rivalries, controversies and alliances. During the bootleg wars of the 1920s, more than 1,000 gangsters were killed in New York. Arnold Rothstein, big-time gambler, businessman, politician, pawnbroker, fixer, and corrupter, attempted to bring order and reason to the extreme competition and chaos prevailing in New York's bootlegging business. "Rothstein's main function," according to his biographer Leo Katcher, "was organization. He provided money and manpower and protection. He arranged corruption—for a price. And, if things went wrong, Rothstein was ready to provide bail and attorneys." Beginning in the fall of 1920, Rothstein bankrolled the activities of Irving Wexler (better known as Waxey Gordon), Frank Costello, William V. "Big Bill" Dwyer, Louis "Lepke" Buchalter, Albert Anastasia, and John T. Noland (alias Jack "Legs" Diamond), whose gang contained such future luminaries as Charles "Lucky" Luciano and Arthur Flegenheimer (Dutch Schultz). By 1923 it was clear to Rothstein that one man could not control bootlegging in New York City, and so he concentrated on other areas of illicit activity, such as narcotics (Katcher, 1959:170).

Following Rothstein's murder in 1928, John Torrio became banker and financier for underworld enterprises in New York. He also worked quietly behind the scenes to organize and rationalize the illicit alcohol business in New York and along the East Coast, just as he had done in Chicago in the early 1920s. In large part through Torrio's talents as diplomat, the largest bootlegging groups in the northeastern United States settled their differences and agreed to share the liquor being smuggled in as well as to divide the market and its profits among themselves. The association was made up of Lucky Luciano's forces (including Joe Doto, or Adonis, and Frank Costello), the Meyer Lansky–Benjamin "Bugsy" Siegel gang, Philadelphia's Nig Rosen, Longy Zwillman of Newark, "King" Solomon of Boston, Rhode Island's Daniel Walsh, Yasha Katzenberg of New York, and the John Torrio–Frank Zagarino group. (Dutch Schultz headed one of the largest bootlegging gangs in New York City, but refused to join with his competitors.) This combination "controlled the importation and sale of liquor in the New York metropolitan area, Boston and vicinity, Rhode Island, Connecticut, New Jersey, and the Philadelphia metropolitan area," according to a U.S. Internal Revenue Service investigative report. Furthermore, "a commission had been formed in Canada by the various liquor interests and they only authorized the sale and export of liquors to these areas when it was destined to members of the Big Seven organization. As the combination grew it had eleven or twelve members, all big and substantial smugglers of liquor." The association functioned until 1933. During its existence "it was all-powerful in its particular field, enforcing its rules by the most drastic racketeer methods." Prices were fixed by the association, which also limited each member as to the amount of liquor he could purchase in Canada and smuggle into the United States. Torrio's share was approximately 5,000 cases of whiskey or its equivalent in bulk per month (U.S. Internal Revenue Service, 1920s, 1930s).

## THE CORRUPTION OF PUBLIC MORALS

Although bootleggers engaged in an illegal enterprise, millions of otherwise honest and law-abiding citizens fully supported, even demanded, this service. The consuming public, in effect, became willing accomplices in the widespread violation of the U.S. Constitution. Paradoxically, bootleggers were, in the popular mind, glamorous and mysterious benefactors, and not corrupters of public and private morals.

The hypocrisy of Prohibition was a corrosive agent. It permitted Al Capone and other underworld figures to self-righteously maintain that their function was deliberately misunderstood or misrepresented by law enforcement authorities and the media. As Capone piously claimed: "I make my money by supplying a public need. If I break the law, my customers, who number hundreds of the best people in Chicago, are as guilty as I am. The only difference between us is that I sell and they buy" (Sinclair, 1964:220). If, as Calvin Coolidge claimed, "the business of America is business," then Capone and his peers were in tune with the spirit of the age because they were businessmen—very successful businessmen, in fact. However, the price paid by the nation and its citizens for the services offered was far greater than the millions of dollars reaped by syndicate criminals between 1920 and 1933.

Prohibition overburdened the criminal justice system and undermined respect for the nation's laws. Until the administration of Herbert Hoover (1929–1933), no serious effort was made to enforce what had become a very unpopular law. The morale and sense of self-worth of law enforcement agents was severely eroded during the 1920s.

The lesson which the young are traditionally supposed to be taught —that crime does not pay—was clearly proven to be false. Crime paid very well, and everyone knew it. Not only did profits obtained from illegal liquor sales enrich criminals almost beyond belief, but they provided the capital to expand syndicate activities into new fields of enterprise, as well as to make possible the purchase of political protection, and even to buy a certain degree of respectability. The open flaunting of wealth and influence by syndicate members, combined with the apparent inability of enforcement agencies and the courts to "bring the wrongdoers to justice," created a pervasive disrespect for the law.

## EXPANSION AND DIVERSIFICATION

The groundwork for the criminal syndicates of the post-World War II era was laid during Prohibition. Many of what we now regard as traditional fields of illegal enterprise gained a powerful impetus during the 1920s and early 1930s. The most obvious was, of course, bootlegging. During the era of the "Noble Experiment," the manufacture and sale of alcoholic beverages became the underworld's biggest money-maker, supplanting gambling, which had held this position since at least the 1870s. Bootlegging is still a money-making activity for criminal syndicates, but a variety of other items, including furs, cigarettes, and electrical appliances, have supplanted alcohol. In fact, any scarce or heavily taxed item holds potential for illegal profit, but bootlegging has, since World War II, played a relatively minor role in the overall operations of criminal syndicates. Other ventures, which were overshadowed during the 1920s and early 1930s, have more than made up for the decline of bootlegging. These include labor and business racketeering, loansharking, and the traffic in narcotics. Even the long-established business of gambling gained new importance with the discovery of the large profits to be made from the numbers racket (also referred to as "policy"), while the much discussed and lamented movement by organized crime factions into legitimate business began during Prohibition. In addition, a number of new money-making enterprises have been tapped, including arson for hire, credit card and real estate frauds, and the pornography business, plus the theft and sale of securities.

The syndicates emerged from World War II in a strong position. During the war, the criminal entrepreneurs catered to public cravings for a wide variety of illegal services and commodities then in short supply. Such items as gasoline, meat, automobiles, tin, and rubber were provided, for a price. In addition to black market operations, the war proved to be a boon to underworld gambling ventures. People played the numbers and flocked to horse and dog tracks, gambling casinos, and bookmakers. Black market and gambling operations continued into the post-war era, and underworld syndicates maintained a tight grasp on both.

By the early 1950s gambling once again had become syndicate crime's greatest source of income, bringing in an estimated $20 million a year with annual net profits of approximately $7 million. Although most of the money came from such illegal operations as slot machines, bookmaking, and policy, illicit entrepreneurs also discovered the opportunities offered by legal gambling in Nevada (U.S. Senate *Second Interim Report*, 1951).

When Bugsy Siegel's creation, the "fabulous Flamingo Hotel," opened in December 1946, it appeared to be a $6 million miscalculation. As events soon proved, it was a stroke of genius. Unfortunately for Siegel, he did not live to bask in the glory or to enjoy the material benefits of his vision. On June 20, 1947 Siegel was murdered in Los Angeles, apparently on orders from East Coast and Midwest syndicate leaders who believed he had misused their money. Meyer Lansky and Frank Costello of New York; Cleveland leaders Moe Dalitz, Sam Tucker, Thomas J. McGinty, and Morris Kleinman; Hyman Abrams of Boston; New Jersey's Joseph "Doc" Stacher; Pete Licavoli of Detroit; Miami's Edward Levinson; Isadore "Kid Cann" Blumenfeld of Minneapolis; and Chicago's Tony Accardo, as well as numerous other syndicate leaders, quickly recognized the opportunities in Las Vegas and invested (either openly or through fronts) in the casino-hotels that sprang up during the 1950s. In the process they turned Las Vegas into the most lucrative gambling spa in the world (Browning and Gerassi, 1980).

By 1967, when the U.S. President's Commission on Law Enforcement and Administration of Justice presented its findings on the extent of organized crime in the United States, profits from illegal wagering on horse races, lotteries, and sporting events totaled at least $20 billion a year, of which criminal syndicates received perhaps $6 or $7 billion. The financial returns from gambling are still substantial. For example, in 1978 New York City police estimated that one Italian crime family in the city, the Vito Genovese family, netted more than $100 million annually just from New York–New Jersey area bets on pro football's Super Bowl (U.S. President's Commission, 1967; *Washington Post*, January 16, 1978).

Howard Abadinsky, in *The Criminal Elite*, argues that the syndicate's involvement in bookmaking and numbers "is usually as a provider or capital at usurious rates of interest, or 'licensing' the operation— essentially an extortionate relationship." This is the case, Abadinsky believes, because bookmaking and numbers require a good deal of skill in order to achieve any significant level of success" (Abadinsky, 1983: 129–30).

Labor and business racketeering, which attracted some underworld interest during the 1920s, was by the following decade a major source of syndicate income as well as a means to enter legitimate business and organized labor. As it developed in the 1920s and 1930s, it became "a system whereby, through the creation of a so-called trade association, by the connivance, cooperation or control of a labor union, and the use of the strongarm squad, a process of shaking down merchants or other industrialists was smoothed out to machine efficiency (Thompson and Raymond, 1940:219).

In the following years racketeering grew to such proportions that the U.S. Senate Permanent Subcommittee on Investigations under the chairmanship of Senator John McClellan conducted a three-year inquiry into corrupt practices in labor-management relations. Conditions were found to be so serious that in 1959 Congress passed the Landrum–Griffin Act, which assigned to the U.S. Department of Labor a major role in the campaign to reduce if not remove syndicate crime's influence in labor unions. In 1978 the Senate subcomittee published the findings of a new investigation. In it Senator Charles Percy observed, "It is now all too apparent that labor-management racketeering has not disappeared in the 20 years since those hearings." Percy noted that the corrupt practices of racketeers "rob the union rank and file of their hard-earned rights and benefits. They force the American consumer to pay a duty tax to racketeers for essential goods and services. In effect, consumers and laborers alike are subsidizing organized crime" (U.S. Senate, 1978:6).

Since the 1930s loansharking has been another major illicit enterprise for criminal organizations. Simply stated, loansharking involves lending money at a higher rate of interest than is charged by legal lending institutions. Interest rates demanded by loan sharks vary from one to 150 percent a week, according to the size of the loan, the potential for repayment, the intended use of the money, and the relationship between borrower and lender. Customers are willing to pay exorbitant interest rates because they are considered to be poor credit risks by legitimate lenders. Customers include bettors and bookmakers who borrow to pay gambling losses, as well as small businessmen with cash flow problems, and narcotics users who need the loan money to buy drugs.

A study conducted by the Russell Sage Foundation in the mid-1930s found that the gross annual income from loansharking in New York City was in excess of $10 million. Three decades later the President's Commission on Law Enforcement judged the loansharking business to be "in the multi-million dollar range," and noted that its profit margins are higher than those obtained from gambling operations (*New York Times*, December 4, 1935; U.S. President's Commission, 1967:189).

During the 1960s criminal syndicates demonstrated their versatility when they tapped a new source of revenue: stolen securities. Although Italian organizations played a prominent role, "a number of other groups, syndicates and combinations of criminals in a loosely organized confederation" participated extensively in the crimes. Securities generally were obtained in one of two ways: either through inside operators in banks or stockbrokerage houses, or by theft of registered mail at airports. In 1971 a congressional committee found that stolen securities were disposed of "through confidence men, stockbrokers and attorneys of shady reputation, fences, and other persons who have the ability, technical knowledge, skill, and contacts to sell the securities or to place them advantageously as collateral in financial transactions." The U.S. National Crime Information Center estimated the value of government

and private securities stolen in 1970 to be at least $227 million, a figure
other authorities considered to be short of the mark (U.S. Senate, 1971:2–5).


## THE GOLDEN AGE OF SYNDICATE CRIME

In recent decades criminal entrepreneurs have devoted increasing attention to legitimate business. There is some disagreement among authorities as to whether this focus represents an effort to use profits obtained
from illegal activities as a means to infiltrate and corrupt legitimate enterprises, or is instead an attempt on the part of upwardly mobile criminal
entrepreneurs to leave a sordid life and gain respectability. In this regard,
Michael Maltz likens syndicate penetration of legitimate business to efforts made by American business leaders of the Gilded Age (the so-called
"Robber Barons") to legitimize the huge fortunes amassed by highly
questionable means. Maltz also observes that "the alternative to [syndi-
cate] penetration of legitimate business is the reinvestment of the ill-
gotten gains into the same criminal enterprises, which may cause greater
social harm" (Maltz, 1976:83).

In the early 1950s, the Kefauver Committee, which strongly endorsed the theory that criminals entered legitimate business in order to
launder money made from illicit activities or to corrupt legitimate businesses or businessmen, noted the presence of syndicate figures in "approximately 50 areas of business enterprise." These included advertising,
appliances, the automobile industry, banking, coal, construction, drug
stores and drug companies, electrical equipment, florists, food (meat,
seafood, dairy products, groceries, cheese, olive oil, fruits), the garment
industry, the import-export business, insurance, the liquor industry,
news services, newspapers, the oil industry, paper products, radio sta-
tions, ranching, real estate, restaurants, the scrap business, shipping,
steel, television, theaters, and transportation (U.S. Senate, *Third Interim
Report*, 1951).

The desire to "go legitimate" has continued to the present. A congressional investigation in 1980 found that profits obtained from illicit
enterprises are, "over time," invested in legitimate businesses that
cover "the whole gamut of our private enterprise system." The committee found that businesses infiltrated through the use of "laundered"
profits cover some 70 areas of economic activity and include "liquor,
transportation, entertainment, sports, hotels and motels, brokerage
houses, labor unions, insurance companies, construction firms, vending
machines, the food industry, trade associations, trucking, waste collection, parking lots, garment manufacturing, resorts and casinos, holding

and finance companies, and real estate development." An estimated 85 percent of the syndicate criminals in the United States have invested at least a part of their "ill-gotten gain" in legitimate business ventures (U.S. Senate, 1980:13).

A significant portion of the enormous profits accruing to criminal organizations has in recent years come from the traffic in illegal narcotics. According to Howard Kohn, the Washington director of the Center for Investigative Reporting, by the early 1980s the underworld's earnings from cocaine, marijuana, amphetamines, heroin, barbiturates, and other illegal drugs "amount by DEA's [Drug Enforcement Administration] estimate to a total of $80 billion a year in unreported business transactions" (Kohn, 1983:80). Contrary to popular belief, this is not a recent phenomenon but dates from at least the 1920s or '30s. Nevertheless, the illegal narcotics business has taken on significantly greater importance in the years since World War II.

In 1974 *Newsday* published a 32-part report that traced the flow of narcotics from the poppy fields of Turkey to the streets of New York. The Pulitzer Prize winning investigative study noted that New York is the center of America's heroin industry, with more than half of the industry's customers believed to be residents of the five boroughs, along with many of the suppliers, wholesalers, retailers, and street peddlers. "In dollar terms, it may be one of the city's biggest industries, with annual sales of $1 billion or more." Control of the business has shifted over the decades from Jewish criminals, in the 1920s and '30s, to Italians in the '40s and '50s. In the late 1950s, however, a new federal conspiracy law went into effect permitting prosecution of bosses who never actually handled the drugs. "Shortly afterward, around 1960, the five New York families prohibited their members from dealing in narcotics." The decision was apparently based·in large part on the fear that those given long prison terms would become informers in order to lighten their sentences. Not all Italian syndicate members moved out of the narcotics business, but an opportunity was created for Cuban groups to move in. Although they faced competition from American blacks, the Cubans enjoyed an important advantage. As *Newsday* observed, the Cubans "had connections throughout Latin America and Europe, the sources of the drugs" (*Newsday*, 1974:198–200).

By the 1970s, still other groups had entered the narcotics trade. As early as 1972, federal agents warned of the increasing involvement of South Americans, as well as the emergence of South Florida as a major center of drug traffic. Thus, a May 1, 1972 article in the *New York Times*, based on information attributed to "federal law enforcement officials," maintained that "enterprising Frenchmen, South Americans, Puerto

Ricans, and Cuban refugees are turning southern Florida into the premier American entry point for smuggled heroin and cocaine.'' This situation reflected the increasing use of South America as a stopover and dispersion point for European-refined heroin as well as ''the growing popularity of South-American-grown cocaine in the United States and an infusion of new Latin elements in the high-profit, high-risk business (*New York Times*, May 1, 1972).

In recent years a number of groups, some well established and some new to the competition, have joined the wild scramble for narcotics dollars. Colombians acquired expanded roles during the 1960s and early 1970s, both as producers and couriers for other distribution networks, and in trafficking and distribution of the Colombian-grown or processed marijuana and cocaine in the United States. Until 1979, outlaw motor-cycle gangs such as the Hell's Angels, Bandidos, Pagans, and Outlaws were viewed by authorities mostly as ''local nuisances,'' but they now display ''all the characteristics of the more traditional organized crime groups. They also have a formal, recognized rank structure that deline-ates authority and privilege.'' In addition to drug trafficking, the motor-cycle gangs are involved in welfare frauds, auto and motorcycle theft, and murder. Even the venerable Italian syndicates, which, according to a *Wall Street Journal* article, ''once viewed motorcycle gangs with con-tempt,'' now make ''increasing use of them for arson, extortion and contract killings'' (U.S. Senate, 1980:18; *Lexington Leader*, September 2, 1981: *Wall Street Journal*, January 11, 1984).

While the outlaw bikers have been compared by the press to the Italian criminal syndicates, a confederation of drug smugglers, pimps, pornography peddlers, burglars, car thieves, and killers-for-hire operat-ing in Florida, Georgia, Alabama, Virginia, Tennessee, Kentucky, and other Southern states has been dubbed the ''Dixie Mafia'' by law en-forcement authorities (*Louisville Courier-Journal*, December 19, 1982).

The complicated nature of syndicate crime, especially in narcotics traffic, led a U.S. Senate subcommittee to conclude that ''there is no one specific ethnic stereotype that is synonymous with 'organized crime.' The composition of organized crime syndicates varies from place to place, from year to year, and from drug to drug'' (U.S. Senate, 1980:61). It must be emphasized that Italian syndicate leaders are not encouraging the changes that are taking place in the world of illicit enterprise, nor are they pleased with these changes. Rather, they have made strenuous efforts to maintain the status quo, but as the most highly publicized and visible element in the underworld they have found this to be a difficult, though certainly not an impossible, task.

Pressure from law enforcement agencies making effective use of the

Racketeer Influenced and Corrupt Organizations (RICO) statute enacted by Congress in 1970, the advancing age of syndicate leaders, and an inability to attract new local talent, combined with increasing competition from blacks, Hispanics and others, may signify the beginning of the decline of the Italian-American syndicates in the narcotics traffic, and perhaps in other fields of criminal activity. Increasingly, Italian syndicates have found it extremely difficult to attract able, intelligent, ambitious Italian-Americans of the younger generation. As a result they have found it necessary either to import eager young toughs from Sicily or to hire motorcycle gang members or other outsiders for needed manpower in the scramble for narcotics dollars (Pileggi, 1973; *Newsday*, 1974).

Although the Italian syndicates are not as powerful as they once were, the organizations are far from dead. It is clear that both the Italian syndicates and their new competitors will continue to prosper by supplying and exploiting the seemingly endless need of the American public for illegal products and services.

## References

Abadinsky, Howard (1983). *The Criminal Elite: Professional and Organized Crime*. Westport, CT: Greenwood Press.

Browning, Frank and John Gerassi (1980). *The American Way of Crime*. New York: Putnam.

Burns, Walter Noble (1931). *The One-Way Ride*. Garden City, NY: Doubleday, Doran & Co.

Chafetz, Henry (1960). *Play the Devil: A History of Gambling in the United States from 1492 to 1955*. New York: C.N. Potter.

Chicago Crime Commission (1919). *Bulletin* 6 (October):1.

———— (1920s, 1930s). Records on file at the commission's offices in Chicago.

"Dixie Mafia Thrives on High Stakes Crime in Bullish Sun Belt" (1982). *Louisville Courier-Journal* (December 19).

Engelmann, Larry D. (1971). "O Whiskey: The History of Prohibition in Detroit." Ph.D dissertation, University of Michigan.

Katcher, Leo (1959). *The Big Bankroll: The Life and Times of Arnold Rothstein*. New York: Harper.

Kohn, Howard (1983). "Cocaine: You Can Bank on It." *Esquire* 100 (October):80.

Landesco, John (1968). *Organized Crime in Chicago*. Chicago: University of Chicago Press.

Maltz, Michael (1976). "On Defining 'Organized Crime.' " *Crime and Delinquency* 22 (July):83.

"Menace . . . Today's Motorcycle Gangs Rival the Mafia, A" (1981). *Lexington Leader.* (September 2).

Messick, Hank (1967). *The Silent Syndicate.* New York: Macmillan.

*Newsday* (1974). *The Heroin Trail.* New York: Signet.

Peterson, Virgil W. (1952). *Barbarians in Our Midst: A History of Chicago Crime and Politics.* Boston: Little, Brown and Co.

Pileggi, Nicholas (1973). "Anatomy of the Drug War." *New York Magazine* 6 (January 8):36.

Sinclair, Andrew (1964). *Era of Excess: A Social History of the Prohibition Movement.* New York: Harper & Row.

Sullivan, Edward Dean (1930). *Chicago Surrenders.* New York: Vanguard Press.

Thompson, Craig and Allen Raymond (1940). *Gang Rule in New York: The Story of a Lawless Era.* New York: Dial Press.

U.S. Internal Revenue Service (1920s, 1930s). Intelligence Unit Investigative Files. Washington, DC.

U.S. President's Commission on Law Enforcement and Administration of Justice (1967). *The Challenge of Crime in a Free Society.* Washington, DC: U.S. Government Printing Office.

U.S. Senate (1951). *Hearings Before the Special Committee to Investigate Organized Crime in Interstate Commerce.* Part 9. 81st Congress, Second Session. Washington, DC: U.S. Government Printing Office. (Also known as the reports of the Kefauver Committee.)

———— (1951). *Second Interim Report of the Special Committee to Investigate Organized Crime in Interstate Commerce.* 82nd Congress, First Session. Washington, DC: U.S. Government Printing Office.

———— (1951). *Third Interim Report.* 82nd Congress, Second Session. Washington, DC: U.S. Government Printing Office.

———— (1971). *Hearings Before the Permanent Sub-Committee on Investigations of the Committee on Government Operations. Organized Crime—Stolen Securities.* 92nd Congress, First Session. Washington, DC: U.S. Government Printing Office.

———— (1978). *Hearings Before the Permanent Sub-Committee on Investigations of the Committee on Government Operations. Labor Management Racketeering.* 95th Congress, Second Session. Washington, DC: U.S. Government Printing Office.

———— (1980). *Hearings Before the Permanent Sub-Committee on Investigations of the Committee on Government Operations. Organized Crime and Use of Violence.* 96th Congress, Second Session. Washington, DC: U.S. Government Printing Office.

# La Cosa Nostra in Drug Trafficking

## Peter A. Lupsha

*Despite La Cosa Nostra's denials of involvement in drug traffick-*
*ing in the U.S., a review of the published record indicates con-*
*tinuous involvement by all major crime families. The national La*
*Cosa Nostra commission's ban on drug trafficking by its members*
*apparently had some impact in 1948–1959, but was increasingly*
*ignored as drug profits soared in subsequent decades.*

"In my Family, some activities were clearly considered out-of-bounds.
I did not tolerate any dealings in prostitution or narcotics" (Bonanno,
1983:149).

"Well, Jimmy, like you told me when I was made, it's against the
rules."
"I know, I know . . . but the rules are broken all the time" (Demaris,
1981:402).

There is much to be gained by a historical and contemporary examination of the role of La Cosa Nostra (LCN) in the drug trade. First, little has
been done to develop an overview of the role played by Italian-American
crime groups in drug trafficking in the twentieth century. Second, patterns and understandings that may appear from examining one group's
activity over time may help us understand patterns in other groups.
Third, La Cosa Nostra, despite recent setbacks and generational shifts,
still plays a major role in organized crime and the drug trafficking crime
matrix in the United States today. Further, La Cosa Nostra's involvement
in drug trafficking underscores the theoretical limitations of Donald
Cressey's "Corporate-Bureaucratic" model of organized crime, and the
need to synthesize this model with the kinship and patron–client
models of Ianni and Albini.

Most important, LCN members' loudly proclaimed unwillingness to

31

engage in the drug matrix is not just a cover, or act of disinformation for the public and law enforcement, it is also an indicator of their moral posturing to themselves and myth systems. Yet an analysis of La Cosa Nostra's participation in drug trafficking reveals the falsity of their self-images and claims to moral rectitude, acceptability and honor.


## LUCKY LUCIANO AND MEYER LANSKY

There is no easy way for the student of organized crime to collect and corroborate empirical data for testing hypotheses. He must work like an archeologist with fragments and pieces, scattered shards which only gradually can be fitted together to form a mosaic that casts light and understanding on our past.

An example of this process is the case of Charles La Gaipa. In 1944, the U.S. Bureau of Narcotics was developing a case against a New York–California–Mexico narcotics ring led by Salvatore Maugeri. The undercover agent in that investigation found himself dealing with Charles La Gaipa of Santa Cruz, California, who later disappeared and is presumed dead (U.S. Treasury, 1950). In the early 1920s, La Gaipa was an associate of Vito Genovese. In June 1923, Genovese brought La Gaipa to meet Charles "Lucky" Luciano, who was a key lieutenant to Joseph Masseria and beginning to make money in bootlegging. La Gaipa needed $20,000 to finance a heroin shipment. According to Luciano, this would return $150,000, of which he would get 60 percent. On June 5, 1923, Luciano was arrested carrying several samples of the heroin over to Joe Adonis's house in Brooklyn for testing.

Nor was this the first narcotics incident on Charles Luciano's record. Seven years earlier he had been arrested carrying a half-dram of heroin on the same New York City street and sentenced to one year at Hampton Farms Penitentiary (Gosch and Hammer, 1974). Thus, Luciano, who is thought by many analysts to be a founding father of Italian-American organized crime, La Cosa Nostra, had an active history in narcotics trafficking (Lupsha, 1981).

After being deported to Italy in 1946, Luciano began diverting legally produced heroin from the legitimate Italian market to his colleagues in the United States (Gosch and Hammer, 1974; Pantaleone, 1966). But by the late 1940s he had, with the assistance of Don Calogero Vizzini, head of the Sicilian Mafia, established a regular network of laboratories for processing morphine base from Turkey, via Lebanese exporters, in Sicily. One factory, opened in Palermo in 1949, operated without incident through April 11, 1954 (Clark and Horrock, 1973; McCoy, 1972;

Charbonneau, 1976). With the assistance of Meyer Lansky, whose European tour of 1949–1950 enabled Luciano's organization to establish ties with the Corsican Mafia, Luciano gained access to a new network of contacts which controlled the criminal activities in Marseilles. Then for the next decade Marseilles and other parts of France became the processing centers for near pharmaceutical-quality heroin passing along the various networks of La Cosa Nostra crime families, and affiliated groups —Sicilian, Corsican, Calabrian, Canadian, South American and Cuban— into the United States.

Meyer Lansky, like Joseph Bonanno, regularly denied any connections to drug trafficking (Eisenberg, Dan and Landu, 1979). Lansky, however, was heir to the legacy of Lucky Luciano, as a 1951 memo of the U.S. Bureau of Narcotics and Dangerous Drugs reveals (McCoy, 1972). A review of Lansky's history shows that he always had close ties to those engaged in trafficking drugs. His early mentor was Arnold Rothstein, whose fortune was based on drugs and gambling (Gosch and Hammer, 1974; Eisenberg, Dan and Landu, 1979). Lansky was an associate of Louis "Lepke" Buchalter, Harry Stromberg, and Saul Gelb, all of whom had long careers as international narcotics traffickers. Thus, Lansky, throughout his life, was close to men who made fortunes from drug trafficking, whether in La Cosa Nostra or in associated Jewish organized crime groups (Messick, 1971).

## BONANNO FAMILY

Charles "Big Nose" La Gaipa remained in the narcotics trade. Nicolo Gentile recalls going to his boss Vincenzo Mangano in the early 1930s and saying that he had the opportunity to "associate myself in the affairs of Charles La Gaipa." Mangano agreed that Gentile could take part in the drug trade as long as he, his consigliere Joe Biondo, and Albert Anastasia shared in the profits (Gentile, 1947:179). Gentile was arrested in New Orleans in a U.S. Bureau of Narcotics crackdown that netted 75 traffickers from New York to Texas.

The involvement of Gentile and the Mangano "borgata" (a word suggesting "community" that is a more accurate term than "family" for referring to LCN groups like Bonanno's), implicates a second of the major New York City La Cosa Nostra families in narcotics trafficking, as well as individuals believed to have had ties to the traditional Unione Siciliana—an organization Humbert Nelli (1976:134–35) describes as "the largest, most influential Italian fraternal group in . . . [Chicago]." (See also Tyler, 1973.) Their involvement with drugs also directly contradicts Joseph Bonanno's recollections:

Mangano and Gagliano too were considered conservatives. We were the Tories of the Commission and for almost thirty years our views prevailed.

We were the most tradition-bound, and our philosophy reflected our Sicilian roots. For example we steadfastly opposed such immoral enterprises as prostitution and narcotics trafficking (Bonanno, 1983:161).

Bonanno is contradicted by other sources too. In his memoirs, he fails to mention his own underboss, Carmine Galante, whose participation in narcotics trafficking is well documented. Nor does Bonanno mention Vincent and Pepe Cotroni, who were Carmine Galante's major suppliers of heroin (Buse, 1965; Charbonneau, 1976). More recently, Salvatore Catalano, underboss of the Bonanno family just prior to Carmine Galante's murder in 1979, was tried for his role in the "Pizza Connection" drug case (Dintino, 1983).

## GENOVESE FAMILY

The Genovese family can also be added to the list of New York La Cosa Nostra families engaged in narcotics trafficking, and the experience of Genovese soldier Joseph Valachi is instructive (U.S. Senate, 1963:632–40). Around 1952 Valachi was approached by Salvatore Shillitani to join in a narcotics enterprise. When 15 kilos of heroin arrived by ship in New York, the profits were divided among Vito Genovese and his associates (Maas, 1969; U.S. Senate, 1963:35–356).

In 1957, an informant named Nelson Cantellops told New York City police of meetings he had attended in which Genovese and his capos planned the takeover of South Bronx rackets and elimination of unauthorized drug dealers there. Genovese, who was supposed to wait outside in the car, joined in the discussion. That mistake cost him 15 years in prison and his career in La Cosa Nostra (Buse, 1965; Hanna, 1974).

After the death of Genovese in 1969, the family leadership passed first to Philip Lombardo, and then to Frank Tieri, whose capos continued to deal in drugs. A 1977 New York City Police intelligence report lists eight members of this family among its top one hundred major narcotics violators. Members of this family were said to be major suppliers for key black trafficking organizations, such as the Leroy "Nicky" Barnes group in Harlem. (Dominick Cappolla of the Genovese-Tieri group and his associate, Lusiano Leggio of Sicily, were linked to Leroy "Nicky" Barnes.) But they were not alone in maintaining the hand of La Cosa Nostra in trafficking. Carmine Tramunti, who replaced Thomas Lucchese as head of that family, was directly involved in narcotics, as were six of his capos in the late 1970s (New York City, 1977–78).

Thus, all major La Cosa Nostra families in the New York City area participated in drug trafficking over long periods despite the supposed prohibitions against La Cosa Nostra involvement in this enterprise.

## THE "LAW" AGAINST DRUG TRAFFICKING

Joseph Valachi notes that "In 1948 there was a law passed in our family" (Salerno and Tompkins, 1969:108). Valachi is referring to a decision by Frank Costello to ban drug trafficking by members of his borgata. According to Valachi, Costello made this decision because of the realization that heroin trafficking was looked down upon by the public and that this activity spurred the Bureau of Narcotics into hot pursuit (Maas, 1969). The Iannis, in their discussion of the Lupollo family, indicate that one member of the family was sent to Florida because the family was "so furious with him" for his association with a drug trafficker (Ianni and Reuss-Ianni, 1972:145). Salvatore "Bill" Bonanno goes even further, noting that his father was so against narcotics trafficking that he once vowed he would put his men in the ovens of his bakery if they were caught in the trade (Talese, 1971).

There were several less stringent ways that La Cosa Nostra tried to enforce this prohibition. Valachi reports that in families where heroin was officially outlawed a member arrested for drug trafficking was ineligible for financial help from the borgata. He also notes that Tony Accardo's Chicago family added a carrot to the stick, paying each member who had been in trafficking $200 a week to get out of the business (Maas, 1969). Annelise Anderson suggests that in some families these strictures were successful; only four members of the Philadelphia Bruno family were arrested for narcotics during the 1950s (Anderson, 1979:245). Other analysts have argued that the Narcotics Control Act of 1956 also had an influence on these prohibitions, as did the conviction of Vito Genovese (Maas, 1969; see also Homer, 1974).

A number of families, however, simply never went along with this rule. The Lucchese family was heavily involved in narcotics trafficking throughout the late 1940s and 1950s, while the Magaddino family of Buffalo is said to have paid lip-service to the rule but not enforce it (Maas, 1969). Other families, like the Bruno group, simply licensed outside crime groups, such as Greek gangs, to carry out this enterprise under a contract and fee arrangement with them (Wallace interview, 1982). This arrangement offered high profits and, often, few risks to the "franchiser."

In times of financial need and crisis, few members of organized crime were going to stay out of this lucrative trade. For example, an FBI microphone recorded a conversation between New Jersey organized crime boss Samuel de Cavalcante and Anthony Russo on May 24, 1965:

De Cavalcante: You know Frank [Cocchiaro] is a rough guy that I have to watch. Frank would do heist jobs [armed robberies] if I'd let him.

Russo: Sammy, do you know how many friends of ours are on heists?

De Cavalcante: They can't support themselves.

Russo: Do you know how many guys in Chicago are peeling [safe-cracking]? Do you know how many friends of ours in New York that made it peeling? What they gonna do? Half these guys are handling junk [narcotics]. Now there a [Cosa Nostra] law out that they can't touch it. They have no other way to make a living so what can they do? (Federal District Court, 1969:F241–43.)

According to New York City organized crime expert Ralph Salerno, La Cosa Nostra looked into the "soft" drug market in amphetamines during the early 1960s, but rejected entry because of insufficient profits and unstable distribution networks. Then, after the Federal Drug Abuse Control Amendment of 1965 altered the supply structure and availability of amphetamines, while demand remained high, they decided to invest in the enterprise (Salerno and Tompkins, 1969). This may have provided some outlets for family members to increase their earnings, but from what we now know this was minimal. It did, however, increase the interaction between La Cosa Nostra members and other crime groups such as outlaw motorcycle gangs that directly engage in drug trafficking. Thus, in 1982, Raymond Martorano and his bodyguard Frank Vadino were sentenced in the Eastern District of Pennsylvania for conspiring to import 250 gallons of P2P from Europe at a cost of $500,000. Martorano was a close associate of Angelo Bruno, and had been put in charge of the Philadelphia family's drug activities by Bruno's successor, Philip Testa. The chemical was to be used by outlaw motorcycle gangs to produce some 2,000 pounds of methamphetamines with an estimated value of $20 million dollars wholesale (Wallace correspondence, 1982).

What can be concluded, then, about the supposed prohibition on drug trafficking laid down by the La Cosa Nostra national commission? All evidence indicates that from 1948 to 1959 the commission edict against engaging in the drug trade was, at least in part, accepted by most of the families. The breakdown of this prohibition may be attributed to the vast profits of the narcotics trade, the loss of power to rival criminal organizations who filled the vacuum created by the edict, and to internal changes, often generational, occurring in La Cosa Nostra itself.

## NEW GROUPS AND NEW DIRECTIONS

Possibly because of the prohibition on drug trafficking, or the increasing public demand for drugs such as marijuana and cocaine—in which the Italian-American organized crime syndicates were not heavily invested in the 1960s and 1970s—other groups came to the foreground in narcotics trafficking (Wallance, 1981; Lupsha, 1983). While La Cosa Nostra groups never left the business completely, their contacts and expertise were primarily in the heroin matrix. Since this was no longer the prime drug of choice, the LCN lost market shares to Asian, Mexican and Oriental organizations. By the late 1970s, however, one could clearly say that La Cosa Nostra had reestablished the Sicilian drug trafficking connection. The murder of Carmine Galante by Sicilian Mafiosi illegally brought to the U.S. (dubbed "Greenies") can be seen as a turning point in restoring this link ("Mafia Boss . . .," 1983; *Organized Crime Digest*, 1985).

Thus, when economist and organized crime expert Peter Reuter wrote that:

> Little evidence exists that the Mafia is intimately involved in either cocaine or marijuana markets, and their role in heroin is far from dominating . . . (1983:183)

he failed to recognize one of the new directions taken by La Cosa Nostra. Various branches and subgroups of the Mafia have been involved in both cocaine and marijuana trafficking and, at the time Reuter wrote his book, the "Pizza Connection" was busy importing some $1.6 billion in heroin via LCN-controlled pizza parlors throughout the United States. Many of these outlets, besides serving as points of transmission and wholesaling of heroin, gave safe haven to "Greenies" on their way to bigger things with the mob (*Narcotics Control Digest*, 1984; Pennsylvania Crime Commission, March 1980). Similarly, cousins of Carlo Gambino with close ties to Sicily were arrested for importing heroin in 1980 (Pennsylvania Crime Commission, March 1980).

In addition to the reemergence of the direct Sicilian connection through the "Greenies," La Cosa Nostra groups also attempted to extend their influence in drug trafficking to South America via the financing of non-Italian trafficking groups such as the Charga brothers, "The Company" and others, as well as having their own younger more aggressive members enter the trade. The Charga brothers, associated with Syrian–Lebanese groups that controlled organized crime in El Paso, Texas, were involved with associates of the Raymond Patriarca LCN family in sending marijuana freighters to New England (Cartwright, 1984). "The Company" worked with Santos Trafficante Jr.'s organization in Tampa, Florida to ease logistical problems in marijuana trafficking (Greenshaw, 1984).

Another of the new trends in LCN drug trafficking is expansion beyond the traditional heroin market into all forms of drugs. For example, in 1983 the New Jersey State Police noted that Florida-based Anthony Accetturo of the Lucchese family, and his associate Michael Taccetta, were actively engaged in the cocaine trade between Florida and New Jersey (U.S. Senate, 1983:138–139). In 1984, the U.S. Senate Permanent Subcommittee on Investigations heard about Ronald Carabbia, a capo in Cleveland's Lonardo/Licavoli LCN family, and Carabbia's brother Orlando, who was indicted for smuggling and distributing marijuana (U.S. Senate 1984:371). And in April 1985, Joseph Bonanno, Jr., pleaded guilty to minor charges in a cocaine conspiracy case (*Organized Crime Digest*, May 1985).

In addition, U.S. Attorney Rudy Giuliani noted that:

> Traditionally groups from Little Italy (Manhattan's Lower East Side) dealt in heroin and other groups in cocaine. But these two groups were working together supplying each other with heroin and cocaine. It shows that drug rings are no longer confining themselves to one drug. [*Organized Crime Digest*, September 1984:5.]

When in October 1984 the "Pizza Connection" was broken by the defection of Sicilian La Cosa Nostra leader Tommaso Buscetta, it was found that Buscetta, while heavily involved in heroin, had been exporting cocaine from Brazil since 1980 (House, 1984). While Brazilian police believe he was still in the process of establishing ties to countries like Bolivia and Peru, there can be no doubt that this La Cosa Nostra figure was also involved in the cocaine trade.

By 1985 it appeared that even though La Cosa Nostra was facing major pressures from law enforcement, and increased strength and competition from a variety of organized crime groups, it continued to be engaged in drug trafficking, and any earlier prohibitions against this trade had been buried with the old leaders who created them. While La Cosa Nostra is likely, in the short term, to falter from these pressures, and to expand further into legitimate business and entertainment, it is also likely that its role in narcotics trafficking will continue. Its dominance will not be as complete as in the days of Charles Lucky Luciano—in part because of new competition—but neither will it carry the moral stigma that some of the old bosses attached to it. Therefore, although organized crime groups may alter their strategies, and the ways in which they are protected from law enforcement, La Cosa Nostra will not simply abandon the drug trade for moral or any other reasons so long as consumer demand and vast profit opportunities in that enterprise remain.

We have seen in this chapter the tensions and the strategies that one traditional criminal organization has engaged in concerning a single crime matrix generally considered to be morally abhorrent. Bonanno's reluctance to write of Carmine Galante or the Cotroni brothers, as well as Fratianno's failure to mention the Dragna family, may in part be based on their shame regarding their involvement in drug trafficking. In addition, we have seen how organizational strategies to limit—some say to monopolize—this traffic at the top have affected the organization, its membership, and cohesion.

La Cosa Nostra is an evolving organization. Many of these patterns of evolution involved its extent and types of participation in drug trafficking.

## References

Anderson, Annelise (1979). *The Business of Organized Crime*. Stanford, CA: Hoover Institution Press.

Bonanno, Joseph (1983). *A Man of Honor: The Autobiography of Joseph Bonanno*. New York: Simon and Schuster.

Buse, Renee (1965). *The Deadly Silence*. Garden City, NY: Doubleday.

Cartwright, Gary (1984). *Dirty Dealing*. New York: Atheneum.

Charbonneau, Jean Pierre (1976). *The Canadian Connection*. Ottawa, Can.: Optimum.

Clark, Evert and Nicholas Horrock (1973). *Contrabandista*. New York: Praeger.

Demaris, Ovid (1981). *The Last Mafioso: The Treacherous World of Jimmy Fratianno*. New York: Times Books.

Dintino, Justin J. (1983). *The Structure of Organized Crime in New Jersey*. New Jersey State Police report prepared for the U.S. Senate Judiciary Committee, February 16.

Eisenberg, Dennis, Uri Dan and Eli Landu (1979). *Meyer Lansky: Mogul of the Mob*. New York: Paddington Press.

Federal District Court, Newark, NJ (1969). *The De Cavalcante Transcripts*. Vol. III.

Gentile, Nicolo (e) (1947). *Translated Transcription of the Life of Nicolo (e) Gentile*. Unpublished manuscript. Palermo, Sicily.

Gosch, Martin and Richard Hammer (1974). *The Last Testament of Lucky Luciano.* New York: Dell.

Greenshaw, Wayne (1984). *Flying High.* New York: Dodd, Mead.

Hanna, David (1974). *Vito Genovese.* New York: Belmont Tower Books.

Homer, Frederic D. (1974). *Guns and Garlic.* West Lafayette, IN: Purdue University Press.

House, Richard (1984). "Mafia Boss' Arrest Reveals Brazilian Cocaine Connection." *Washington Post,* November 22.

Ianni, Francis A.J. and Elizabeth Reuss-Ianni (1972). *A Family Business.* New York: Russell Sage Foundation.

Lupsha, Peter A. (1981). "Individual Choice, Material Culture, and Organized Crime." *Criminology* 19 (May):10–12.

———— (1983). "Networks vs. Networking: An Analysis of an Organized Criminal Group." In: *Career Criminals,* edited by Gordon P. Waldo. Beverly Hills, CA: Sage Publishers. Pp. 59–87.

Maas, Peter (1969). *The Valachi Papers.* New York: Bantam Books.

"Mafia Boss Killed by His Own Men, Government Says" (1983). *Albuquerque Journal* (February 21).

McCoy, Alfred (1972). *The Politics of Heroin in Southeast Asia.* New York: Harper & Row.

Messick, Hank (1971). *Lansky.* New York: G.P. Putnam's Sons.

*Narcotics Control Digest* (1984) 14:8 (April 18):1, 3–8.

Nelli, Humbert (1976). *The Business of Crime.* Chicago: University of Chicago Press.

New York City. Organized Crime Control Bureau (1977–78). *Narcotics Violators Book* (unpaginated).

*Organized Crime Digest* (1985) 6:3 (March):6–7.

———— (1985) 6:5 (May):9.

Pantaleone, Michele (1966). *The Mafia and Politics.* London, UK: Chatto & Windus.

Pennsylvania Crime Commission (March 1980). *A Report of the Study of Organized Crime's Infiltration of the Pizza and Cheese Industry.* St. Davids, PA: Commonwealth of Pennsylvania.

———— (September 1980). *A Decade of Organized Crime, 1980 Report.* St. Davids, PA: Commonwealth of Pennsylvania.

Reuter, Peter (1983). *Disorganized Crime.* Cambridge, MA: MIT Press.

Salerno, Ralph and John S. Tompkins (1969). *The Crime Confederation.* New York: Popular Library.

Talese, Gay (1971). *Honor Thy Father.* Greenwich, CT: Fawcett Publications.

Tyler, Gus (1973). *Crime in America.* Ann Arbor, MI: University of Michigan Press.

e Committee on the Judiciary (1983). *Organized Crin.*
*merica: Hearings Part 1*. 98th Congress, First Session. W.
ington, DC: U.S. Government Printing Office.

˙ ɔ. Senate Permanent Subcommittee on Investigations (1984). *Profile of Organized Crime: Great Lakes Region: Hearings*. 98th Congress, Second Session. Washington, DC: U.S. Government Printing Office.

U.S. Senate Permanent Subcommittee on Investigations of the Committee on Government Operations (1963). *Organized Crime and Illicit Traffic in Narcotics*. 88th Congress, First Session. Washington, DC: U.S. Government Printing Office.

U.S. Treasury, Bureau of Narcotics (1950). *Traffic in Opium and Other Dangerous Drugs for the Year Ended December 31, 1950*. Washington, DC: U.S. Government Printing Office.

Wallace, Frank D. (1982). Organized Crime Division, Philadelphia Police Department. Correspondence, July 7.

_____ (1982). Organized Crime Division, Philadelphia Police Department. Personal interview, February 12.

Wallance, Gregory (1981). *Papa's Game*. New York: Ballantine.

# The McDonald's-ization of the Mafia

## Howard Abadinsky

*From primitive quasi-military units to a system of franchis Italian-American organized crime has evolved into a formidab entity for both competing criminals and law enforcement agencies. The unique structure of Mafia families has enabled a relatively small number of persons to exercise a great deal of power and generate considerable income with a minimum of effort.*

### INTRODUCTION

The structure of Italian-American organized crime has been described as local ethnic groups (Albini, 1971; Anderson, 1979; Abadinsky, 1981) that are best understood in terms of culture and kinship (Ianni and Reuss-Ianni, 1972) and patron-client networks (Albini, 1971; Nelli, 1976; Abadinsky, 1983).[1] These descriptions contrast markedly with the more bureaucratic model posited by Cressey (1969).

According to Cressey, each crime family is hierarchical, with a boss, underboss, *consigliere*, buffers, lieutenants, and soldiers. The boss transmits orders through an underboss whose "position is, essentially, that of executive vice-president and deputy director of the 'family' unit" (Cressey, 1969:113). At the same level as the underboss is a *consigliere*, "a staff officer" who advises the boss but gives no commands or orders. "To reach the working level, a boss usually goes through channels": from underboss to "buffer," to lieutenant or *caporegime*, a person who, "considered from a business standpoint, is analogous to works manager or sales manager" (Cressey, 1969:114). At the street level are soldiers who report to the lieutenants.

Italian-American organized crime has actually moved from more bureaucratic forms to a structure that can best be portrayed as a *franchise*—the "McDonald's-ization" of the Mafia.[2] This modern form of organization has allowed a small number of persons to exert a great deal of influence and amass considerable amounts of income with minimal effort.

43

## ORGANIZATIONAL TRANSITION

At the height of the Prohibition violence in Chicago, Al Capone is reputed to have had more than 700 men under arms, among them some of the most proficient gunmen in the country (Allsop, 1968). Indeed, armed retainers were standard for criminal organizations of many different ethnic groups during the 1920s and 1930s. An informant told Whyte (1961:120) about the racketeers in "Cornerville" (Boston) during the 1930s:

> . . . there's the muscle men. They muscle in to take over a business. There ain't much work for them now. There's the strong-arm men, they protect the business when it gets going. There's the killers. . . . All them men get paid every week, and maybe for some of them there won't be no work for 51 weeks out of the year, but for that other week, there's plenty they got to do.

During the 1930s a Brooklyn-based unit of Jewish and Italian killers, dubbed "Murder, Inc.," was kept on a paid retainer by a combine of leading New York City racketeers (Turkus and Feder, 1951).

Supporting these "armies" were the organization's workers, who actually operated illegal and sometimes legitimate businesses as well. With the demise of Prohibition and the rise of *syndication* (agreements between competing organized crime units), there was a dramatic decrease in the violence associated with organized crime.[3] Many persons employed by organized crime units for "muscle" were no longer needed; they drifted into conventional criminal activity or abandoned crime as a career. This was particularly true of Jewish criminals (Fried, 1980). Among Italian crime units, members who continued in criminal activity had to adapt to major changes in organization, changes that represented a transition from primitive forms of quasi-military units to a mature form of modern organization—the franchise. The individual member could no longer depend on the family for his support. To survive, he had to become an independent entrepreneur who was expected to aggressively seek out opportunities for making money, or go hungry. This form of organizational structure now characterizes contemporary Italian-American organized crime.

## CONTEMPORARY ITALIAN-AMERICAN ORGANIZED CRIME

There are about two dozen Mafia families in the United States located in urban areas with relatively large Italian-American populations, such as

New York, Philadelphia, Detroit, and Chicago. Their history dates back to shortly before the Prohibition era, and their identity as integral units took shape in the 1930s (Nelli, 1976; Bonanno, 1983). The structure that has emerged is relatively simple. At the center is a boss (or *capo*), who is usually assisted by an underboss (or *sottocapo*) and a counselor (or *consigliere*); he is the patron to a number (depending on the size of the family) of captains (or capiregime); a captain usually acts as a patron for a number of "made-guys," the lowest ranking members (sometimes referred to as *soldati*) of a family (Abadinsky, 1981, 1983, 1985). According to law enforcement sources, each family has anywhere from about 10 to 200 members.

The boss will have his own illegitimate and legitimate business enterprises, often in partnership with members of his family or other families. In addition, he will receive a tithe from the earnings of his captains. Each captain will have his own illegitimate, and often legitimate, business operations. He will also receive a tithe from the earnings of the made-guys under his patronage (Abadinsky, 1981).

The made-guy is invariably male and of Italian heritage. He usually has a history that includes such ordinary criminal acts as burglary and robbery, and has exhibited an ability to earn a great deal of money. He often has a reputation for violence, and needs to indicate a willingness to be involved in violent activities, including murder. He will have close friends or relatives who are involved in organized criminal activities. The made-guy, except in unusual circumstances, has undergone an extensive period of testing and probationary status as an associate to one or more respected members of the family. It is not unusual for this period to last more than a decade.

To be "made" or initiated requires a sponsor who assumes responsibility for the initiate. The sponsor will also be responsible for murdering the initiate should he go "sour." Once initiated into the family, the initiate is referred to as a "good fellow" or a "friend of *ours*" (nonmember associates are referred to by their patrons as a "friend of *mine*"), or simply as a "wise-guy." The initiation process is analogous to the southern Italian custom of *compareggio* or *comparatico*. A fictitious kinship is established between the initiate and his family—the *capo* becomes his *padrino* (godfather)—to whom he pledges lifelong fealty and obedience.

Initiation transforms the initiate into *uomo rispettato*, a man who commands respect (Gambino, 1974). He has achieved formal recognition of his criminal skills by an organization of violent men. He has been given a franchise to use his family connections and status as a violent entrepreneur to make money.[4]

## THE FRANCHISE

The made-guy is not an employee of the family, nor does he have a supervisor in the conventional sense of that term. While he has certain (mostly financial) responsibilities to the captain who acts as his patron, the family has no financial obligations to the made-guy, although help may be provided to those in need for a limited period of time. The made-guy is a violent entrepreneur literally on the prowl for money-making opportunities. Not every member of a family is financially successful, however. This was noted in the "De Cavalcante Tapes"⁵ when family boss Sam De Cavalcante had to arrange for *amici nostri* ("friends of ours") in the Gambino family to secure employment as construction laborers. This reality serves to limit membership. "Hungry" members may be tempted to engage in activities that could jeopardize the family, such as competing with other members in their own or another family, or perhaps engaging in high-risk drug transactions.

In a typical pattern, a made-guy will attract non-members (his "crew") who are eager to associate with him, to become "connected." This enables the associate to share some of the status and connections that the family enjoys, and it places the made-guy at the center of an action-based unit for coordinated criminal activities. If the member is able to generate considerable income, he gains status in the family and can become a candidate for *caporegime*. Successful associates, if they are "Italian," become candidates for membership.

The made-guy can utilize the concept of *rispetto* to generate income. More than 50 years ago Cesare Mori (1933:69), a police prefect sent by Mussolini to deal with the Mafia in Sicily, noted that *rispetto* requires:

> . . . a concrete recognition of the prerogatives of immunity belonging to the *mafioso*, not only in his person, but also everything that he had to do with or that he was pleased to take under his protection. In fine, evildoers had to leave the *mafioso* severely alone, and all the persons or things to which, explicitly or implicitly, he had given a guarantee of security.

When the made-guy, our modern urban American *mafioso*, associates himself with a gambling operation it becomes "protected." An independent operation, on the other hand, is branded as an "outlaw"—the made-guy can cause it to be victimized by robbers or raided by the police. Loansharking becomes an easy source of continuing income for the violent entrepreneur. He need only lend his reputation to the enterprise to avoid competitive efforts and ensure timely repayment of debts. For example, in 1985 the author met with a successful bookmaker ("Ben") in the New York City metropolitan area. Ben also ran "Las Vegas Nights" for a variety of charitable organizations. Throughout most of his career, which spanned more than 30 years, he kept a made-guy (he used the term "wise-guy") on his payroll, often a person he had met only once or twice, at a salary of between $200 and $300 a week. What did the made-guy do for this salary? Nothing—he merely lent his name to the enterprise. For example, while overseeing a Las Vegas Night, Ben was accosted by two rough-looking characters who began to slap him around. Quickly recognizing the approach as a shakedown, Ben tried to shout out the name of "his" made-guy, but he had forgotten the name. His partner quickly ran over and began shouting the name. The two men backed off and Ben never heard from them again.

The made-guy is a trusted insider within an elaborate network that links the "worlds" of labor unions, business, and politics to the "underworld" of crime and criminals. Boissevain (1974:24) notes that every person is embedded in a social network, "The chains of persons with whom a given person is in contact." Since contact can be through a chain of persons, an individual can send a "message" to far more people than he actually knows directly. In the world of organized crime, these are the "friends of friends," or *gli amici degli amici*—a descriptive Sicilian euphemism for *mafiosi*. Boissevain (1974:147) points out: "Every individual provides a point at which networks interact. But not everyone displays the same interest in and talent for cultivating relationships with strategic persons for profit."

The made-guy is such a person. He is trusted by those in need of illegal goods or services and by those who can provide them. He can put you in touch with the "right people." He can bridge communication gaps between legitimate and illegitimate worlds, between the police and ordinary criminals, between businessmen and family-connected union officials; he can arrange for the "torching" of a declining business or the disposition of expensive jewelry; and he can truly "get it for you wholesale." He can provide a variety of merchandise at discount prices, acting as a broker between thieves and fences and the business world. When a legitimate businessman hires a made-guy (usually for a "no-show" position), he finds that labor problems or vandalism cease. Through his connections with labor unions the made-guy can assist with opening up new markets for a businessman (see Kwitny, 1979), or restrain market entry and thereby limit competition (see U.S. Congress, 1981).

The made-guy is "safe" to deal with. He has been "certified" by the family. In a world without a formal system of adjudication, he provides a limited type of insurance for those who deal with him, protection against being "ripped off" by other criminals. Working against a made-guy's associate would be regarded as an affront to *uomo rispettato*, and the violent entrepreneur would react violently. If necessary he could reach out to persons in his network who specialize in violence: the enforcers and executioners.

Because the made-guy has access to private violence, he is in a position to police illegal agreements. The importance of this service in the case of restraint-of-trade agreements in the private solid-waste collection industry in New York City is noted by Reuter (et al., 1983:11):

> Racketeers play a continuing role in the operation of this agreement. That role comes mainly through the need to constantly mediate disputes that inevitably arise in a conspiracy that involves the allocation of over 100,000 customers between 300 carters. The "grievance committees" that settle these disputes, using the basic rule that whoever serviced the site first has continuing rights to any customer that occupies that site, includes at least one Mafioso. While there is little evidence of either threats or actual violence, it seems reasonable to infer that the racketeers provide a credible continuing threat of violence that ensures compliance with the rulings of the committees.

Boissevain (1974) points out that a broker requires a great deal of time to manage his network adequately, develop and maintain contacts, provide services that enhance power, and keep well informed; and time is something the made-guy usually has in abundance. He may have a legitimate business used as a tax front and headquarters for his operations, or he may be on the payroll of a legitimate firm or union for a "no-show" or "consultant" position. In any event, he will spend a great deal of time "making the rounds," visiting bars, restaurants, coffee shops, athletic clubs and social clubs. Anyone in need of his services can leave word at these locations. The made-guy is always meeting people, getting or giving information, and scheming. At times he will meet with his patron and provide a brief summary of his activities and a portion of the profits (but unlike bureaucratic entities, written records are eschewed in organized crime; financial accounting is usually haphazard, and the made-guy can easily underestimate his income).

## A CASE STUDY—TONY PLATE

According to law enforcement officials there are between 1,500 to 2,000 members of Italian-American organized crime in the United States. While the case of one made-guy cannot represent this population, it can provide insight into the issues being discussed.

Our subject is Tony Plate (FBI #625476), who was born in New York City on April 2, 1913.[6] He was known by several aliases, including Mr. Glass (an alternate translation of his real surname Piatto), Mr. Schwartz, or simply "TP." Until 1979 Plate was a made-guy in the Gambino family, one of the five families in New York City and reputedly the largest in the United States, with approximately 200 members. Standing about 5'8", slim but muscular, nearsighted and wearing glasses, Plate's criminal record dates back to 1931, although his only felony conviction was in 1936 for armed robbery. He became a member of the Gambino family, then headed by Vincent Mangano, after his release from Sing Sing Prison.

Plate's early activities as a made-guy are not well known, but he did control the illegal lottery (numbers) in the West Harlem section of Manhattan until he was forced out by black operators in the 1960s. Money from the numbers was used to enter loansharking, and Plate became one of the biggest shylocks in the Gambino family. In addition to lending money directly, he had a number of associates who were entrusted with capital, men such as Charlie "Bear" Calise, a 6'4", 260 pound hoodlum used by the Gambino family for assignments involving violence. Calise had associates too—violent individuals who worked for him in his loansharking operations. Plate also invested heavily in the construction of high-rise condominiums and shopping centers in Palm Beach, Broward, and Dade counties in Florida.

In addition to his home on Bay Harbor Island near Miami, Plate enjoyed the use of rooms and facilities, all gratis, at the Carvel Inn in Westchester County, New York, and the Diplomat Hotel in Hollywood, Florida. He was reportedly the "resident" wise-guy for these two business operations. Summers were spent in New York, winters in Florida. During his stay in New York, Plate would trade in his Cadillac for the latest model, again gratis. Plate's influence is illustrated by the following incident: Plate was in a Cadillac dealership getting his car serviced when he noticed that the owner was troubled with some rather severe vandalism—one of Plate's associates had shot up the showroom. Always gracious and helpful, Plate offered his services to the owner, an Italian, as a *uomo rispettato*. The vandalism stopped.

When an associate who was being groomed for membership in the Gambino family said his sister-in-law, a beautician, was in need of employment, Plate again provided his inimitable form of assistance: he walked into the beauty parlor of the Diplomat Hotel and told the manager to hire the new beautician, who would be in to start work the following day. When the manager protested that he did not need another beautician, Plate glared at him and shouted, "Then fire someone!"

Plate's associates, who included politicians and ranking police officers in New York and Florida, were often his guests at hotels and motels in Florida where the attractions included free food and drinks, in addition to attractive young women eager to please Plate's friends. Plate was known for his ability to handle legal situations for persons in the Gambino and other families. He was also known as a bad-tempered and extremely violent individual who threatened debtors with bottles and spit in their faces. After Charlie "Bear" Calise was discovered stealing funds from Plate and providing information to the authorities, his body was found on July 7, 1974 with bullet holes in the mouth, ears, and eyes. Plate himself disappeared in 1979 and is presumed dead.

Plate did not report to a captain (*caporegime*). Instead, in contrast to the bureaucratic mode, he avoided this level in the hierarchy and reported directly to the family underboss, Aniello DellaCroce, with whom he shared some of his considerable earnings. The extent of Plate's financial success can be gauged by a disclosure he made at a bail hearing (*United States of America v. Aniello DellaCroce and Anthony Plate*, 79-6035) shortly before he disappeared in 1979: a home valued at $135,000, $135,000 in certificates of deposit, $12,000 in savings. He said he had been unemployed for two years, but actually had never had legitimate employment.

## IMPLICATIONS

The system of franchising outlined above makes Italian-American organized crime a particularly difficult entity to confront, both for criminals who would compete with its enterprises and for law enforcement agencies.

The absence of armed retainers by Italian-American families during more recent times leads Reuter (1983:xi) to conclude: "My analysis suggests that the Mafia may be a paper tiger, rationally reaping the returns from its reputation while no longer maintaining the forces that generated the reputation." Reuter theorizes that having established a dominant position, an unchallenged monopoly of force, the Mafia can depend on its fearsome reputation, an asset that can be substituted for personnel costs that would be incurred by maintaining armed forces. He states that the challenge to the Mafia in the black and Hispanic communities "has not generated any effort by the Mafia to assert control through superior violence" (1983:136). Reuter further theorizes that this may be based upon the lack of available force, or simply the result of a cost-benefit analysis, since excessive violence attracts law enforcement attention and is bad for business in general. Reuter is right and wrong.

The Mafia is in the business of making money with a minimum amount of effort; a "wise-guy" is someone who can be financially successful without working at a legitimate job. Although a necessary resource for doing business, violence must be kept to a minimum since it can incur significant costs. Homans (1974:213) points out: "An effective threat of punishment is much cheaper than punishment itself, although should actual punishment never occur, the actual threat may become incredible. The trick is to keep the actual use of force as infrequent as possible." Minimizing violence does not make the Mafia a "paper tiger." Indeed, the unique qualities of its organizational structure make challenges by other criminals quite difficult.

Reuter (1983) notes that challenges to the Mafia outside of black and Hispanic communities have not been noticeable.[7] An appreciation of the business structure of organized crime provides an explanation. The Mafia is often "invisible"; that is, members usually avoid operating illegal enterprises such as gambling, or marginal businesses like "topless" or "strip joints." Instead, they "license" such enterprises, receive payments for restricting market entry and competition, or provide no service —simple extortion. (In Chicago these are referred to as "street taxes.") How would a competing group set out to deal with this operation? The most obvious method would be a direct attack on family members. But they do not reside, meet, or otherwise assemble in significant numbers, and they may be unknown to anyone except persons intimately involved in the local criminal underworld. The decentralized nature of the organization would render a frontal assault unproductive. While a number of members and associates could be killed here and there, the net effect would be analogous to punching an empty paper bag.

Any group with the temerity to undertake this challenge would require the resources to sustain an "army" in the field for an indefinite time. Older members such as Tony Plate would probably head for their condominiums in Florida, Arizona, and California, but remaining behind would be a cadre of assassins whose sole function would be to murder those making the challenge. Associates would see this as an opportunity to prove themselves, and thus qualify for membership, and the "troops" would be sustained by family resources. While Reuter questions the martial skills of modern *mafiosi*, in Chicago a number of assassins have been police officers and deputy sheriffs. Reuter (1983:133) also notes: "Large numbers of young men in major American cities are willing to accept paid employment as violent disputants." Rational criminals with martial skill would be inclined to side with an organization that already has proven its staying power—the Mafia—rather than take a chance with a seemingly reckless new group. Add to this the continuing importation of tough young Sicilians by a number of families, and the sum total is far from a "paper tiger."

On the other side of the ledger, law enforcement activities against Italian-American organized crime are similarly hampered by the unique structure. The bulk of the income of a particular family member is independent of any other member, and the incarceration of a member does little except cut off non-member associates. If they can find a new patron/made-guy, their business activities will continue as usual. In other words, the family is more than the sum of its parts and is not significantly weakened by the elimination of any of its members—as long as there are other prospective members waiting to be "made," to be recipients of a *franchise*.

## Notes

1.  For a discussion of the definition of organized crime, see Albanese (1985); Abadinsky (1985).

2.  In the modern business sense of the term, a franchise is a grant from a parent company to a dealer of the right or license to sell a product or service. For example, a 20 year Burger King license costs $40,000, for which the franchisee gets the right to display the Burger King sign and sell products designed by the parent company.

3.  For example, from 1930 to 1949, in the New York City metropolitan area, there were 109 known Italian-American "gangland" murder victims, and almost half were killed before 1933 (Block, 1975). In Chicago, from 1925 to 1934, there were 547 "gangland" murders; from 1935 to 1954 there were 145 (Peterson, 1969).

4.  Borrowed from Blok's (1974) reference to Sicilian *mafiosi* as violent peasant entrepreneurs.

5.  During the 1960s, the FBI (illegally) bugged the office of Sam ("The Plumber") De Cavalcante, boss of a small New Jersey family, for almost four years. On June 10, 1969, as a result of De Cavalcante's trial, some of the results of the bugging were made public.

6.  Information on Tony Plate is from a number of sources, including newspapers, the *Congressional Record*, criminal informants, and federal law enforcement officials.

7.  Cleveland may provide an exception. There, the Licavoli family was challenged by a non-Mafia group with some success. However, the family had been weakened by the reluctance of the leadership to "make" new members.

## References

Abadinsky, Howard (1981). *The Mafia in America: An Oral History.* New York: Praeger.

_____ (1983). *The Criminal Elite: Professional and Organized Crime.* Westport, CT: Greenwood Press.

_____ (1985). *Organized Crime.* 2nd ed. Chicago: Nelson-Hall.

Albanese, Jay (1985). *Organized Crime in America.* Cincinnati: Anderson.

Albini, Joseph L. (1971). *The American Mafia: Genesis of a Legend.* New York: Appleton-Century-Crofts.

Allsop, Kenneth (1968). *The Bootleggers: The Story of Prohibition.* New Rochelle, NY: Arlington House.

Anderson, Annelise (1979). *The Business of Organized Crime.* Stanford, CA: Hoover Institution Press.

Block, Alan A. (1975). *Lepke, Kid Twist and the Combination: Organized Crime in New York City, 1930–1944.* Ph.D dissertation, Department of History, University of California at Los Angeles.

Blok, Anton (1974). *The Mafia of a Sicilian Village, 1860–1960: A Study of Violent Peasant Entrepreneurs.* New York: Harper and Row.

Boissevain, Jeremy (1974). *Friends of Friends: Networks, Manipulators and Coalitions.* Oxford: Basil Blackwell.

Bonanno, Joseph (1983). *A Man of Honor: The Autobiography of Joseph Bonanno.* New York: Simon and Schuster.

Cressey, Donald R. (1969). *Theft of the Nation.* New York: Harper and Row.

Fried, Albert (1980). *The Rise and Fall of the Jewish Gangster in America.* New York: Holt, Rinehart and Winston.

Gambino, Richard (1974). *Blood of My Blood: The Dilemma of Italian-Americans.* Garden City, NY: Doubleday.

Homans, George C. (1974). *Social Behavior: Its Elementary Forms.* New York: Harcourt Brace Jovanovich.

Ianni, Francis A.J. and Elizabeth Reuss-Ianni (1972). *A Family Business: Kinship and Social Control in Organized Crime.* New York: Russell Sage Foundation.

Kwitny, Jonathan (1979). *Vicious Circles: The Mafia in the Marketplace.* New York: Norton.

Mori, Cesare (1933). *The Last Struggle With the Mafia.* London: Putnam.

Nelli, Humbert S. (1976). *The Business of Crime.* New York: Oxford University Press.

Peterson, Virgil (1969). *A Report on Chicago Crime for 1968.* Chicago: Chicago Crime Commission.

Reuter, Peter (1983). *Disorganized Crime: The Economics of the Visible Hand.* Cambridge, MA: MIT Press.

Reuter, Peter, Jonathan Rubinstein, and Simon Wynn (1983). *Racketeering in Legitimate Industries: Two Case Studies. Executive Summary.* Washington, DC: U.S. Government Printing Office.

Turkus, Burton B. and Sid Feder (1951). *Murder, Inc.: The Story of "The Syndicate."* New York: Farrar, Straus and Young.

U.S. Congress (1981). Permanent Subcommittee on Investigations. *Waterfront Corruption.* Washington, DC: U.S. Government Printing Office.

Whyte, William Foote (1961). *Street Corner Society.* Chicago: University of Chicago Press.

# Violence in Organized Crime: A Content Analysis of the De Cavalcante and De Carlo Transcripts

## Kip Schlegel

*Violence in the context of organized crime has received consider-able scholarly attention. For the most part, this attention has re-mained theoretical, focusing on violence as a rigidly structured, rational response to both internal and external pressures that threaten the organization. So far, there has been little objective empirical data to support these characterizations. This study rep-resents an effort to test empirically some of the assumptions about the nature and function of violence in organized crime by exam-ining information obtained from electronic surveillance of two organized crime groups: the De Cavalcante family and the De Carlo family.[1]*

### THEORIES OF VIOLENCE IN ORGANIZED CRIME

Violence in Italian-dominated organized crime groups has been charac-terized as an "indicator as well as consequence of ever-increasing rational-ity in the Weberian sense" (Block, 1980:202). Cressey (1969:59), for ex-ample, notes that violence plays an important role as a means of "mini-mizing the degree of conflict and maximizing the degree of conformity among members." According to Cressey, the function of violence is so crucial as to merit specific structural positions within the organization hierarchy. The "enforcer," for example, is responsible for making the arrangements for killing and injuring members as well as nonmembers of the organized crime group. The "executioner" is responsible for carry-ing out the actual violence. Both positions are "functional equivalents

55

of the criminal law, whereby punishments are to be imposed 'justly' and in a disinterested manner'' (Cressey, 1969:167).

Cressey's work represents the first real effort to reach some systematic understanding of Italian-dominated organized crime in America. A more detailed and elaborate account of the role of violence in these groups comes from a later study in 1969 by the U.S. Commission on the Causes and Prevention of Violence. Using Cressey's work as a foundation, the staff report entitled *Violence and Organized Crime* separates the functions of violence in organized crime into two primary categories: internal and external violence (Ianni and Reuss-Ianni, 1976).

Internal violence is used for three primary purposes: (1) to enforce security; (2) to stop the threat of rebellion; and, (3) to control competition from other organized crime groups. The use of violence to enforce security is primarily intra-familial. It serves as a means of disciplining those members who do not obey orders, or who fail to live up to their responsibilities. The use of violence to stop the threat of rebellion can be both intra-familial and intra-organizational. If unrest in a particular Cosa Nostra family cannot be contained by the boss, outside members might intervene through the use of violence to eliminate any possibility of the spread of rebellion to other families. Violence as a means of controlling competition is external to the extent that it is directed at those who are not members of Cosa Nostra, but internal in that it is used against other organized crime groups. The use of violence for such a purpose is generally considered a last resort, and takes place only when the organized crime group's "relative position in the community of organized criminals is weak enough to be challenged" (Ianni and Reuss-Ianni, 1976:269).

External violence refers to the use or threat of force against individuals who are not associated with the organized crime group in any criminal capacity. External violence has its roots in extortion, and is generally applied when organized crime groups take over a legitimate business venture. The group then uses "all the techniques of violence and intimidation which are employed in its illegal enterprises" in order to drive out competitors (Ianni and Reuss-Ianni, 1976:268).

To date, there has been little objective research to test these theories about the role of violence in organized crime groups. In one of the few studies of a particular organized crime group, Francis Ianni and Elizabeth Reuss-Ianni (1973) found that the use of violence in the "Lupollo family" in New York was both infrequent and apparently more spontaneous than a rational response to outright disobedience of authority that threatened family honor. They write (p. 165):

Rules of conduct are meant to be enforced, and a system of sanctions always has to be established. Previous studies of organized crime have stressed coercive sanctions or the allocation of punishments including death, as the principal means of control in the Italian-American criminal syndicates. it would be naive to suggest that such sanctions do not exist in the Lupollo family, but this study did not produce any evidence of them.

The Iannis' finding may, of course, be an artifact of their research method. If one asks a member of an organized crime family about the extent and use of violence, one may question the validity of the response. On the other hand, the Iannis' finding may portray the role of violence more accurately than theories emphasizing the bureaucratic structure of organized crime. More empirical research is needed to test theories that now float without anchor. In this study, using information from wiretaps of the De Carlo and De Cavalcante organized crime groups, theories of violence in organized crime are put to test.

## THE DATA BASE

During the course of four years, from early 1961 to the summer of 1965, the U.S. Federal Bureau of Investigation (FBI) planted 98 wiretaps and eavesdrop devices at offices and restaurants believed to be frequented by members of organized crime (*New York Times*, 1969). Although it is impossible to know all of the locations of those listening devices, or exactly how many organized crime groups were under surveillance, at least five of them are known: the National Cigarette Service in Providence, Rhode Island, owned by Raymond Patriarca, who was considered the boss of the New England organized crime family; the Best Sales Company in Clinton, New Jersey, owned by Gerardo Catena, believed by law enforcement officials to be the substitute boss for Vito Genovese, at that time in prison; the Penn-Jersey Vending Company, operated by Angelo Bruno in Philadelphia; the Kenilworth Plumbing and Heating Company in Kenilworth, New Jersey, originally operated by Nick Delmore, who was considered to be the boss of the central New Jersey crime family (after Delmore's death in 1964, both the business and the criminal activities were assumed by Sam De Cavalcante); and finally, the Mountainside Restaurant in Mountainside, New Jersey, where Ray DeCarlo, the underboss to Catena, had his office.

The surveillance procedure was as follows: The FBI established "tech-rooms" (camouflaged offices near the "bugs") where agents monitored loudspeakers connected to microphones. When an agent heard a conversation of interest he would record the discussion and mark it down in a log. Each evening an "agent-in-charge" would review the recordings, keeping those considered relevant and erasing the rest. The transcripts themselves are a combination of verbatim conversations, a copy of the logs recording what was overheard, and government memoranda summarizing relevant information from both. Unfortunately, the memoranda also contain information that is not found in either the log or in the verbatim conversations. As will become evident, this presents a considerable problem for data analysis.

Because the written log is an incomplete synopsis and does not contain sufficient information for study, it has been excluded. The content analysis will focus on the verbatim conversations and the government memoranda that appear throughout the transcripts.

## METHODOLOGY

References to violence were categoried from the verbatim accounts and non-replicated information from the memoranda in the De Cavalcante and De Carlo transcripts. A violent reference was defined as any information that directly or indirectly refers to the use or threat of force. The violent references were then divided into six categories.

### 1. Reference to Past Murder

A reference to a past murder includes any mention that a killing took place. Examples range from a single and rather meaningless sentence such as "the guy that got killed" (FDC, 1969, 7:112) to more detailed and colorful accounts such as this conversation between Tony Boiardo and Ray De Carlo (FDC, 1969, 1:8):

Tony: How about that time we hit the little Jew . . .
Ray:   As little as they are they struggle.
Tony: The Boot hit him with a hammer. The guy goes down and he comes up. So I got a crow bar this big, Ray. Eight shots in the head. What do you think he finally did to me? He spit at me and said [obscene].

### 2. Reference to Planned Murder

A reference to a planned murder involves a detailed discussion concerning the procedures that were to be used in killing someone. The following conversation is an example (FDC, 1969, 7:80–83).

Bob: This guy—hasn't he got any suspicion about anything?

Sam: No. Have the hood up. Like you're putting oil or something in there.

Bob: I'll keep the money and whatever else he brings. And I'll give Louie the clothes . . . shoes . . .

Sam: Okay . . . tell Frank not to be a cowboy . . . Make sure . . . [whispers].

Bob: [inaudible]

Sam: Don't want to use a rope? You don't want to use a rope?

Bob: He says he feels [or kills] better with his arm. He can handle it better with his arm.

Sam: Well, you have a rope ready anyhow.

Bob: That's right—he showed me. He nearly wrecked me.

## 3. Reference to Past Beating

A reference to a past beating differs from a reference to a past killing only to the extent that no death was involved. Any use of physical force except one leading to a death was considered a beating. The following is an example from a memorandum account (FDC, 1969, 4:102):

> . . . Bobby asked Sam if it were not true that Sam "slapped this guy around a couple of times." Sam acknowledged that he had, in fact, claimed to have hit him across the face with a pistol, breaking his teeth.

## 4. Reference to Planned Beating

The following are examples of references to planned beatings. The first is taken from government memoranda on Ray De Carlo (FDC, 1970, 3:79):

> Prior to Martone's arrival at the meeting Poverino suggested to Rega that they had given Martone ample time to collect the money and recommended that Martone be beaten up in order to show him they meant business.

and the second on surveillance of Sam De Cavalcante (FDC, 1969, 7:106):

> Kay was described as a Jewish builder in the shore area who always builds non-union and refuses to pay off for being allowed to do so. Sam suggested that they take this matter up with Pussy [Anthony Russo] first. Cochiaro was in favor of a beating.

## 5. Reference Involving Specific Threat of Death

This category includes any information containing a direct threat of death against a specific individual. The following example is from a conversation between Larry Wolfson, De Cavalcante's business partner, and Harriet Gold, Wolfson's sister and company secretary (FDC, 1969, 2:8):

> Larry: He [Bobby Basile] says to me, "you know, one of these days, cousin or no cousin, I ain't gonna hold back," I said, "hold back what?" "I'm gonna exterminate that lousy weasel like he didn't exist."

## 6. Reference Involving Specific Threat of Beating

References involving specific threats of beatings range from comments such as, "Lou replied emphatically that he could [talk to Jimmy Arley] and furthermore would break his head if requested" (FDC, 1969, 4:331), to De Cavalcante's warning to an individual named Jerry: "If you ever come to see me and say you're gonna do something to somebody outside of busting his head or leg—you're never gonna walk out of this office" (FDC, 1969, 4:372).

A typology of violent references allows for a better understanding of the nature and extent of violence in organized crime. Yet it says little about the functions of such violence. For this reason, this study is also concerned with the individuals who made the reference (termed the violent reference *subject*) as well as with the person to whom the violence was directed (the violent reference *object*). Each reference was coded according to whether the subject or object was: (1) De Cavalcante or De Carlo; (2) a De Cavalcante or De Carlo group member; (3) a member of a different organized crime group; or, (4) an individual who was not a member of organized crime. These categories provide a basis for analyzing the internal and external functions of violence in these groups.

It is still difficult, however, to determine the exact nature of the violence from these factors alone. Assuming for the moment that violence is not necessarily the product of organizational or entrepreneurial rationality, it is of interest to find the extent to which acts of violence were unrelated to the activities of the criminal organization. Consequently, each reference was classified into instances where the references were known to be related to criminal activity and those which, based on the evidence, appeared to be personal. A related objective was to uncover the justification behind each violent reference. Each reference was thus categorized according to whether the act was vindictive or coercive: Did the act occur as a means of revenge for a previous act, or was it a means of forcing the victim to comply with the wishes of the subject?

## FINDINGS

### 1. Frequency of Violence in the De Cavalcante and De Carlo Transcripts

The De Cavalcante transcripts contain 71 references to violence (see Table 1). Although these references cannot be considered accurate gauges of the actual use of violence, they do provide a general picture of the extent of violence used.

**Table 1**
Violent References in the De Cavalcante Transcripts

| Category | Frequency | Percent |
|---|---|---|
| References to past murders | 15 | 21.1 |
| References to planned murders | 2 | 2.8 |
| References to past beatings | 7 | 9.8 |
| References to planned beatings | 0 | 11.2 |
| Specific threats of death | 22 | 30.9 |
| Specific threats of beating | 17 | 23.9 |
| Total | 71 | 100 |

Interestingly, six of the 15 references to murder in the De Cavalcante transcripts occur in a single conversation. (That conversation is repeated in the De Carlo transcripts, thus accounting for six of 27 references to murder in those transcripts.) The conversation, which took place in De Carlo's office in March 1963, indicates quite clearly that murders did occur. Here is an excerpt from that discussion (FDC, 1969, 1:14).

Sam: Ray, you told me years ago about the guy where you said, "Let me hit you clean."

Ray: That's right. So the guy went for it. There was me, Zip, and Johnny Russell. So we took the guy out in the woods and I said, "now listen." Zip had the . . . on him and I said, "leave him alone, Zip." I said, "look" . . . was the guy's name. I said, "you gotta go, why not let me hit you in the heart and you won't feel a thing." He said, "I'm innocent, Ray, but if you gotta do it. . . ." So I hit him in the heart and it went right through him.

Sam:    The guy we were supposed to [inaudible]. They were spit-
        ting all over me you know.
Ray:    Oh well, I would have left him on the street.
Sam:    They didn't want them on the street. They didn't want the
        rest of the mob to know that permission. . . .
Ray:    But I mean a guy like Willie [Willie Morretti] "We like you
        and all, but you gotta go. You know it's an order, you gave
        enough orders."

This conversation refers to a previous discussion concerning the
killing of Willie Morretti. De Carlo and De Cavalcante were disgusted
with the way in which he was killed. They continue:

Ray:    You got five guys there, you talk to the guy. Tell him this is
        the lie detector stuff. You tell him, "You say you didn't say
        this . . ."
Tony:   How many guys are you gonna con?
Ray:    Well, if you don't con him then tell him. Now like you got
        four or five guys there in the room. You know they are gonna
        kill you. They say, "Tony Boy [Anthony Boiardo] wants to
        shoot you in the head and leave you on the street or would
        you rather take this, we put you behind your wheel, we
        don't have to embarrass your family or nothin" that's what
        they should have done with Willie. . . .

Three of the 15 references to murder indicate that De Cavalcante or
a De Cavalcante associate was responsible for the murders. Of these
three references, only one clearly indicates that a murder actually took
place. Ironically, one reference involves a plea made to De Cavalcante
by an associate that he was not responsible for a murder in spite of persistent rumors throughout the group to the contrary (FDC, 1969, 8:146).
    Similarly, there are surprisingly few references to past beatings in
the De Cavalcante transcripts. Of the seven references in this category,
only one describes a beating in any detail—the previously cited reference (FDC, 1969, 4:102) in which De Cavalcante admitted having hit an
individual "across the face with a pistol, breaking his teeth."
    Of the 115 references to violence (see Table 2) in the De Carlo tran-
scripts, 27 involve references to past murders, while another 21 involve
references to past beatings.[2] As with the De Cavalcante data, the majority
of references to murders did not involve De Carlo or a De Carlo
associate. Only five of the 27 references involved the De Carlo group
directly.[3]

**Table 2**
Violent References in the De Carlo Transcripts

| Category | Frequency | Percent |
|---|---|---|
| References to past murders | 27 | 23.4 |
| References to planned murders | 7 | 6.0 |
| References to past beatings | 21 | 18.3 |
| References to planned beatings | 16 | 13.0 |
| Specific threats of death | 15 | 13.0 |
| Specific threats of beating | 29 | 25.2 |
| Total | 115 | 100 |

At first glance, the 21 references to beatings indicate a substantial number of violent acts. Yet, as with the De Cavalcante references, a closer look reveals that a large portion of the references pertain to only a few acts. For instance, six of the 21 references involve only one individual, a Jewish loanshark named Harold Konigsberg, who was supposedly in competition with De Carlo. Furthermore, of the 21 references only eight involve beatings administered by either De Carlo or people suspected to be his associates.

Since these transcripts were recorded over a period of four years, it does not appear that the actual use of physical violence was extensive. Even where the references are explicit, it is difficult to determine when they took place. It is known, for example, that Willie Morretti was killed in 1951, and that the murder of Albert Anastasia, also mentioned in the transcripts, occurred in 1958. It is possible that a number of other beatings and murders took place at a much earlier time than their reference, thus distorting any notion of the frequency of violent acts. Of course, it is difficult to know with any accuracy who was a member of these groups, and one can be fairly certain that more violence did in fact occur than the instances cited in the recorded conversations. Yet, given the time frame and repetitious nature of the references, it does not appear that actual violence was as prevalent in these two groups during this period as one might presume having casually read the transcripts.

## 2. Threats of Violence

What about the use of threats of violence? From the data in both the De Cavalcante and De Carlo transcripts it appears that words spoke louder than actions. There are 22 specific threats of death and 17 threats of beatings in the De Cavalcante transcripts. The De Carlo transcripts contain 44 specific threat references, of which 15 pertain to murder and 29 to beatings. Among the 22 specific threats of death in the De Cavalcante transcripts, apparently none resulted in actual violence—at least as far as can be discerned from the recorded conversations. Similarly, neither of the two references to detailed plans of murder resulted in an actual killing as far as one can tell from these data. (A subsequent examination of the local newspapers for this time period also failed to substantiate these claims.)

A similar pattern emerges with regard to De Cavalcante threats of beatings. Of those threats for which the object of the violence is identifiable, none are substantiated by the references to actual or planned beatings. It is possible that some may have occurred, since there are two references to beatings in which the object is not identified. Yet, based on the time differences between the threats and the unidentified acts (not less than a year), it is unlikely that the incidents are related.

The De Carlo transcripts contain similar evidence. None of the six detailed plans of murder are substantiated by the references to actual killings. And of the 15 references to threats of death, none go further than talk based on the accounts of actual killings. One slight difference can be found in reference to beatings. A comparison of the references to actual beatings with the detailed plans or threats of beatings indicates that at least three threats were, in fact, carried out.[4]

While many of the threats of violence are not matched by references to actual violence, an analysis of this sort certainly cannot be used to suggest that the beatings never took place. They may well have occurred and simply were not discussed, or they may have occurred after the recording period. Yet, based on this evidence, it appears that threats were not always—it may be said, not usually—carried out. Clearly, some of the individuals recorded in the transcripts were very fearful for their safety. Therefore, the most plausible conclusion to draw from this analysis is that the threat of violence seemed to be an effective means of instilling fear, but only seldomly were threats carried out.

## 3. Function of Violence

Of the 71 references in the De Cavalcante transcripts involving either past killings or beatings, planned killings, or beatings and specific threats of death or beatings, 41 are references made by either De Cavalcante or someone assumed by the FBI to be a De Cavalcante group member. In order to get some idea about the internal control function of violence in organized crime, it is important to look at the seven references directed at individuals assumed to be family members. Six of them were made by De Cavalcante himself, while the seventh involves a personal dispute between two other members. Of the references made by De Cavalcante, all but one refer to criminal activity as opposed to personal disputes. All of the references are coercive in nature, and they are split equally between specific threats of death and specific threats of beatings. With the exception of the one personal dispute between the two members, which did result in a fight, most do not involve actual violence. The following conversation is typical of most of the references and involves a threat to a De Cavalcante group member (FDC, 1969, 1:71).

> Sam: Louie's got the $1,900 dollars in his pocket. I want you to go out of here and if you feel you deserve the whole $1,900 then you can have it. If you feel that these fellows have something coming, then give it to them. . . . Now Louie came here because he had to come here. Now, if you feel you can get along without Louie—he can get along without you. But Jerry, it goes both ways. Don't you ever come to us with no furs either. Or if you're not with us, don't bother anybody that has anything to do with us.
>
> Jerry: Sam, I take an oath on my grandson, who I love so much . . . if through my connections, we can make some money—fine. All I want is a piece.
>
> Sam: But I want to tell you, Jerry. If you ever come to me and say you're gonna do something to somebody outside of busting his leg—you're never gonna walk out of this office.
>
> Jerry: I'm sorry I said that. This would never happen! Believe me.

Is this pattern similar regarding internal control in the De Carlo group? Of the 115 references, 68 are by De Carlo or individuals assumed to be members of the De Carlo group. Of those 68 references, six are directed at individuals who are said to be associates. As with the De Cavalcante transcripts, none of the references involve actual violence. Two of the six involve plans for beatings, while the remaining four are split between specific threats of death and beatings. All the references are related to criminal activity rather than personal motives and, unlike the De Cavalcante data, the majority are vindictive as opposed to coercive. This may seem odd, since most of the references suggest threats rather than actual violence, yet closer analysis reveals that three of the threats concern one individual and appear to reflect momentary anger that subsided over time. As with references in the De Cavalcante transcripts, the majority of these references are found in government memoranda as opposed to verbatim accounts. The evidence from this analysis suggests, then, that violence was seldom actually used as a means of enforcing security and preventing rebellion within either the De Cavalcante or De Carlo organizations.[5]

What about internal violence directed at other organized crime groups as a means of eliminating competition? In order to explore this question it is important to first make a distinction between those organized crime groups assumed to be a part of La Cosa Nostra and those which are not.

Surprisingly, this distinction is of little consequence in the De Cavalcante data since no references fall into either category. It appears that at least with regard to the two principal activities in which De Cavalcante was engaged—labor racketeering and loansharking—violence in any form was seldom used as a means of dealing with competitors.

The references to violence directed toward other groups in the De Carlo transcripts, on the other hand, suggest that violence was one means of maximizing internal control. Of the 68 references, 16 are directed at individuals who were affiliated with other organized crime groups. Of these 16 references, eight are directed at other Cosa Nostra members. The majority of these eight references are related to criminal activity as opposed to personal disputes, and they are split evenly between being vindictive and coercive in nature. The remaining eight references are directed at individuals who apparently operated with other groups or on their own. Interestingly, five of those eight references are directed at a single individual, a Jewish loanshark, "Irving Berlin," who apparently operated in the same territory with De Carlo. The following memorandum is an example of one of the references (FDC, 1970, 2:135):

> On 11/7/62 NK 2251-C* reported that subject [De Carlo], Carl Selesia, and Joe Polverino had Irving Berlin at subject's headquarters where they "slapped him around." At issue appeared to be some derogatory remarks which Berlin allegedly made against De Carlo. Also De Carlo was angered at Berlin's attempts to align himself with other racket figures in various gambling ventures.

The data from the De Carlo transcripts thus suggest that other groups or individuals operated in the same activities and in the same territory, apparently under mutual agreement with De Carlo. Likewise, it appears clear that violence was one means of enforcing those agreements.

## 4. External Violence

External violence refers to the use or threat of force against individuals who were not associated with the De Cavalcante or De Carlo organizations in any kind of criminal activity. It refers primarily to those individuals who were clients in either labor racketeering or loansharking (De Cavalcante's principal activities), or gambling (De Carlo's principal activity, although he was also engaged in loansharking).

Of the 41 references made by De Cavalcante or De Cavalcante associates, 30 are directed at individuals apparently not associated with organized crime except in the role of client. Eight of those 30 references do not contain enough information to make them meaningful. Of the remaining 22, 12 involve conversations pertaining to either labor racketeering or loansharking. Of the six which are labor related, two involve past beatings, one refers to a murder, and three involve either plans for or threats of beatings.

Of the 68 references made either by De Carlo or De Carlo associates, 19 concern individuals not directly associated with organized crime. The majority of those references are directed at individuals who have failed to repay loans made by De Carlo, or who were apparently delinquent on gambling debts. The following is a discussion concerning a delinquent debtor named Joe Green (FDC, 1969, 9:92):

Ray:    He [Green] don't like to pay—you do that—tell him to come up here—I'll hit him another backhand. Leash hit him a slap in the face and he cried like a baby. The yellow Jew—they're all alike. [De Carlo had Green beaten in November 1952.]

Unfortunately, the majority of the references in this category come from government memoranda, which are the weaker and more unreliable of the two data sources. As a consequence, it is difficult to extrapolate much from these data. Had the conversations been kept in verbatim form, it might have been possible to get a better understanding of the tactics used in collecting delinquent debts, the decision to use violence, or alternatives to it.

Although they have little relation to the business of organized crime, there are a number of references to external violence that may tell us a great deal about particular individuals. For instance, one reference involves a discussion about the action to be taken against an associate of De Cavalcante who, in a moment of rage, hit someone in the face with a shovel (FDC, 1969, 7:246, 247). In another conversation, De Cavalcante describes how an associate harassed several teenagers while driving down the street, only to be stopped by the youths several blocks later and clobbered with a baseball bat (FDC, 1969, 8:188). Finally, even De Cavalcante seems to outdo himself when he threatens to kill his brother, threatens to kill his brother's wife, and threatens to kill his business partner's wife (FDC, 1969, 4:330: 7:140: 8:206). Clearly, these threats cannot be taken seriously. Yet, how is one to discern the seriousness of any threat when it comes from the written page? Quite obviously, this is a problem which hinders any analysis of this type (see Schlegel, 1984).

## 5. Structure of Violence

The final analysis involves the structure of violence within these two organized crime groups. Unfortunately, there are insufficient data to determine whether positions such as "enforcer" and "executioner" are evident in these two groups. It appears that an individual named Bobby Basile was involved in violence most frequently in the De Cavalcante group (one actual beating, five planned beatings), and Carl Selesia was involved most frequently in the De Carlo group, having also taken part in one actual being and five planned beatings. This information does not mean, however, that these individuals had any specialized skills for such tasks, other than perhaps being physically suited for such activity, or that they were specifically regarded as the "executioners" of the groups.

## SUMMARY AND CONCLUSIONS

To date, most of the information available on the extent and function of violence in organized crime has been supplied by law enforcement agencies that keep track of such groups. While the information they supply may, in fact, be accurate, there has been little objective research undertaken to bolster our knowledge on the subject. The lack of research is most certainly due to a lack of independent data to scrutinize. Such data may be extracted from the transcripts of surveillance recordings of supposed organized criminals, but these data are not without bias. Agents who record the information inject a bias in what they choose to record and how they describe the events in the memoranda they submit as evidence. Obviously these agents are trained to listen for key words and phrases relevant to pre-existing concepts of organized criminal activity. Those concepts may or may not reflect the reality.

There are a number of other caveats needed about how far one can speculate with the evidence presented here. First, there is absolutely no certainty that the conversations appearing in the transcripts are "typical" of the universe of discussions by these individuals. It could well be that most discussions concerning the planned use of violence took place somewhere other than in the offices where the bugs were located. Second, there are a great number of violent references that simply do not contain sufficient information for reliable classification. Obviously, if we knew more about these references—who was the actual subject, who specifically was the object—the picture of violence might change considerably. Third, and perhaps most importantly, it is very difficult to interpret many of these discussions. For instance, when an individual says on tape, "he got hit," does he mean, "he got punched," "he got shot," or "he lost money on the numbers?"

It should also be taken into consideration that the extent of violence evident in the De Cavalcante and De Carlo transcripts may or may not have been typical of either organized crime in general, or of those two groups at different times.

Given these caveats, the data do provide some interesting pointers about the use of violence in these two groups. First, although there is a fairly large number of references to violence by both these groups, the references to actual violence, either in the form of murders or beatings, involve only a small portion of the total references. Second, threats of violence appeared to play an important role in both families, but the extent to which those threats were made good appears minimal. Third, there is little evidence to suggest that actual violence was used in either group as a means of controlling group behavior, although at times both De Carlo and De Cavalcante were prone to make threats of physical violence when enraged at an associate's behavior. Fourth, there is evidence to suggest that violence, or at least the threat of violence, was used by the De Carlo group as a means of enforcing territorial agreements. The evidence is less clear in this respect in the De Cavalcante group. Finally, although there is little evidence to suggest that clients were coerced into agreements with De Cavalcante or De Carlo, violence, and more often the threat of violence, appear to be means by which agreements between "suppliers" and "customers" were enforced.

## Notes

1. The De Cavalcante and De Carlo transcripts have been selected for study here for two reasons. First, they are the most detailed and extensive wiretap recordings available. Together the two sets of transcripts consist of more than 4,300 pages. The second reason for selecting these data is that they permit clear comparisons. The information was recorded during the same general time period (from 1961 to July 1965), both sets involve organized crime families in New Jersey, and each concerns different organized criminal activities (loansharking and labor racketeering). Although the data are restricted to a particular time period and geographic location and thus probably do not reflect what is occurring in Italian-dominated organized crime today, they do provide an excellent source by which most theories of violence in organized crime may be examined.

2. One must be cautioned not to use the frequencies of violent references to compare the two groups. Given the differences in time

frames, the recording practices, and the amount of time each individual may have spoken into the bugs, it is simply impossible to state that violence is any more or any less prevalent in one organized crime group than the other. However, it may be possible to make some general comparisons regarding the functions of violence within each group by analyzing the references from each data set.

3. Of the five references, two involve separate accounts of the "killing of the little Jew"; one involves an unspecified killing committed by De Carlo (also mentioned in the conversation with De Cavalcante (FDC, 1969, 1:14); one involves the accidental death of an individual who subsequently died of a heart attack after a beating; and the last is a reference containing insufficient information to understand the exact nature of the killing.

4. In early 1964, for example, De Carlo suggested to several associates that they go to an individual named Joe Masher and "bang him around." In a conversation recorded in December of the same year, De Carlo complained that Masher informed the FBI about the beating that was administered to him earlier (FDC, 1970, 4:170: 6:115).

5. There are, however, a number of references to an internal dispute involving the Bonanno family. De Cavalcante believed that unless Bonanno met with the Commission and obeyed their orders, they would have Bonanno killed.

## References

Block, Alan (1980). *East Side, West Side: Organizing Crime in New York, 1930–1950.* Cardiff, Wales: University College Cardiff Press.

Cressy, Donald (1969). *Theft of the Nation.* New York: Harper and Row.

Federal District Court (FDC), Newark, NJ (1969). *Transcripts of Electronic Surveillance of Sam De Cavalcante.* Vols. 1, 2, 4, 7, 8, 9.

_____ (1970). *Transcripts of Electronic Surveillance of Ray De Carlo.* Vols. 2, 3, 4, 6.

Ianni, Francis A.J. and Elizabeth Reuss-Ianni (1973). *A Family Business: Kinship and Social Control in Organized Crime.* New York: New American Library.

_____ (1976). *The Crime Society.* New York: Meridian.

*New York Times* (1969) (June 14:16).

Schlegel, Kip (1984). "Life Imitating Art: Interpreting Information From Electronic Surveillances." In *Critical Issues in Criminal Investigation*, edited by John K. Fairbank. Cincinnati: Pilgrimage Press.

# Part III:
# Strategies for the Control of Organized Crime

# Following Dirty Money: The Kaufman Commission and Organized Crime*

## John Dombrink
## and Malorie Melrose

*The recent U.S. President's Commission on Organized Crime chose money laundering as the subject of its first report. A review of the commission's report and other published information indicates that money laundering is a promising target for prosecution. But laundering is difficult to track, in part because of banking procedures intended to protect the confidentiality of transactions. Administrative and legislative measures will be necessary to bolster enforcement of laws against laundering.*

In the last 50 years, various state and federal crime commissions in the U.S. have struggled with a mandate to define and defeat organized crime. Each of the primary commissions and committees has largely described the prototypical forms of organized crime of their respective eras.

In the 1930s, for example, the Wickersham Commission, appointed by President Hoover, called attention to the effects of Prohibition in corrupting local law enforcement. Most of the social problems associated with organized crime at that time pertained to bootleggers (U.S. National Commission, 1968). During the 1950s, the Kefauver Committee directed much of its investigative effort to tracking illegal gambling operations, their prosperity, and their corrupting influence (Bell, 1962; Kefauver, 1951; W.H. Moore, 1974). Later in that decade, the McClellan rackets committee, concentrating on labor racketeering, undertook an exten-

---

*An earlier version of this paper was presented at the 1985 Annual Meeting of the Academy of Criminal Justice Sciences in Las Vegas, Nevada.

73

sive probe into Teamsters Union operations (Kennedy, 1960; McClellan, 1962; U.S. Senate, 1958).

Next, a 1967 report from the Task Force on Organized Crime of the President's Commission on Law Enforcement and Administration of Justice reiterated many of the concerns of the Kefauver Committee, and emphasized both the illicit goods and business/labor sources of criminal revenues (U.S. President's Commission, 1967). At the same time, the 1967 report concluded that "too little is known about the effects on the economy of organized crime's entry into the business world (U.S. President's Commission, 1967:5; see also Schelling, 1967). As that knowledge increased in the decade after the 1967 report, significant legislation and law enforcement resources were directed to blocking organized crime involvement in legitimate business.

For example, one of the key purposes of the Racketeer Influenced and Corrupt Organizations (RICO) provisions is to detect organized criminal activity in nontraditional areas (Organized Crime Control Act of 1970, Pub. L. No. 91-452). RICO is an effective prosecution tool. However, money laundering has only recently become a qualifying predicate offense under RICO. (See Meeker and Dombrink, 1984.)

The recent President's Commission on Organized Crime—appointed by President Reagan and headed by federal judge Irving Kaufman (hereafter referred to as the Kaufman Commission)—chose money laundering as the subject of its first report (U.S. President's Commission on Organized Crime, 1984). This new emphasis on money laundering by the commission and other law enforcement authorities is based on the presumptions that it will yield more convictions and stiffer sentencing of high-level criminals, especially narcotics traffickers, and that bankers, lawyers and accountants implicated in money laundering may prove more willing than "professional criminals" to become government witnesses (Blau, *et al.*, 1983:133).

## MONEY LAUNDERING: AN OVERVIEW

A definition offered by a team of U.S. Justice Department officials involved in the prosecution of money laundering is useful:

> Laundering involves the hiding of the "paper trail" that connects income or money with a person in order for that person to evade the payment of taxes, avoid prosecution for any federal, state or local offense and obviate any forfeiture of his illegally derived income or assets. While a financial investigation may concentrate on the money involved with crime, and particularly the proceeds, the

criminal basis for the underlying offense is also our primary concern. By addressing the concept of financial crime, and attacking the finances of a criminal enterprise, the predicate crime (e.g., narcotics, gambling, extortion, illegal tax shelters) can be more effectively handled [Blau, *et al.*, 1983:124].

Much of the money laundering in this country has been linked by prominent prosecutors to the drug trade (interview with federal prosecutors, 1984). The potential to make an enormous and immediate return on capital investment is one of the most enticing attractions of the drug trade. However, the successful drug trafficker is faced with the problem of laundering his profits in order to hide their illegitimate source. Thus, the prosecution of money laundering has great potential for targeting those traffickers who are otherwise too adept to be discovered by traditional means (Blau, *et al.*, 1983).

Creating an illusion as to the origin of the organized criminal's money is central to his movement into the legitimate sphere (Karchmer, 1985; Lernoux, 1984). To obscure his illicit income, the organized criminal may engage in many financial subterfuges, including money laundering techniques. Incorporated within the technique of money laundering is the manipulation of financial institutions. The structure of contemporary banking systems helps the money launderer, since the banks often maintain discretionary services that actually contribute to the laundering process. Cashier's checks, for instance, are beneficial to both the money launderer and the financial institution: They enable the organized criminal to invest in legitimate business while obscuring the source of the revenue. Cashier's checks also benefit financial institutions, since they take a long time to clear, allowing a bank to accrue interest upon the amount drawn on the check. Also helpful to money laundering are financial institution policies that permit deposits by customers with unverified identities, or whose funds are of "foreign origin," or who are acting on behalf of foreign companies without power of attorney, or via wire transfers that make laundering virtually impossible to trace (Blau, *et al.*, 1983; U.S. President's Commission, 1967; Lernoux, 1984).

Bank officials who engage in these discretionary practices are generally indifferent to the suspicious nature of laundering transactions. Employees cite a concern for the privacy of the customer as the basis for their failure to question or report suspicious transactions or customers. One major problem faced by those trying to impede laundering techniques is the lack of formalized procedures within banking institutions to deal with money launderers. Many banks find it sufficient to follow the guidelines of the U.S. Right to Financial Privacy Act (RFPA), which states that federal authorities can only investigate dealings of the bank by grand jury subpoena, court order, or written request. The RFPA also requires the bank to notify the customer of the agency's inquiry into their account.

Another problem is that banks are not obligated to respond to information requests from the authorities. The RFPA authorizes a financial institution not to disclose information it believes is protected by the law. However, the financial institution is still subject to civil and criminal liability for its refusal to comply with court orders or subpoenas. Since the bank stands to gain substantial profits from these money laundering practices, there is great incentive not to comply with the authorities' requests. The Right to Financial Privacy Act—which governs Federal investigations but not local regulatory agencies—thus presents procedural obstacles to piercing bank secrecy and impeding laundering techniques (U.S. Senate, 1983).

Another type of financial institution associated with money laundering is the offshore bank, which is often a branch of a U.S. financial institution. These banks are loosely supervised by foreign central bank authorities, and afford the investor the advantage of a tax haven. The advantage to offshore banks is that they are located in countries with very low tax rates, no currency exchange controls, and no regulations governing bank interest. Senate staff investigators have estimated, based on interviews with bankers and police in offshore jurisdictions, that approximately $50 billion is sent offshore annually (U.S. Senate, 1983:15). Though some offshore banks are beginning to relax restrictions on government inquiries, these are still outnumbered by banks offering "blanket secrecy."

Another type of financial institution offering this "blanket secrecy" is the Euro-market, which, because of its less regulated market, is appealing to the organized criminal. As of 1984, the United States had no treaty arrangement with any jurisdiction for exchange of offshore banking and corporate information, which makes these markets attractive to the money launderer. In addition, the United States will not, for reasons of crime and tax loss, impose trade-destroying currency controls, upon Euro-market trading (U.S. Senate, 1983).


## DRUG TRAFFICKING AND MONEY LAUNDERING:
## TWO CASE EXAMPLES

One example from the *Cash Connection* report of the President's Commission on Organized Crime spotlights a money launderer whose career was probably typical of the traditional relationship between Colombian drug traffickers and money exchangers. Isaac Kattan, who was eventually indicted for his role in a money laundering scheme utilizing Miami's Great American Bank, performed money laundering for at least one major cocaine-trafficking organization. Kattan or his couriers would deposit large sums of narcotics proceeds into a "Currency Exchange Corporation" account; the money was then transferred via cashier's check, wire transfer, or check to another bank where Kattan held an account under a false name. The Great American Bank, which laundered more than $94 million between January 1980 and February 1981, assisted by falsifying names of remitters on Kattan's cashier's checks and by failing to file the Currency Transaction Reports mandated by law.

The next stage of the scheme was summarized by the President's Commission on Organized Crime as follows:

> After a series of transactions through foreign tax havens, the U.S. funds would then appear as assets of Kattan's Colombian travel agency, which was also a front for Kattan's Colombian black market money exchange. Kattan would then pay Colombian narcotics traffickers in Colombian pesos, as well as finance the transportation of narcotics from Colombia to the United States [U.S. President's Commission, 1984:41].

For the $6 million deposited at the Great American Bank in a 14-month period of 1980 and 1981 by Kattan's group, Kattan paid a $47,000 "fee" to a loan officer of the bank. Officers and bank employees treated the drug traffickers as valued customers, even when their deposits included a number of counterfeit bills. And Kattan did not perform his service in the dead of night: he and his couriers "always did business openly at GAB, bringing bags and boxes directly to the lobby where the money was counted" [U.S. President's Commission, 1984:41].

In another case developed by "Operation Greenback"—a federal multi-agency investigation of drug trafficking in south Florida—over $8 million was seized by the government and forfeited under civil statutes related to the prosecution of money laundering and drug trafficking activities (21 U.S.C.881(a)(6)). In the case known as "SONAL" (after the names of the bank account seized)—but officially cited as *U.S. v. Four Million, Two Hundred Fifty-Five thousand etc., et al.*, and *U.S. v. Three Million Six Hundred Eighty-Six Thousand, etc., et al.* (762 F 2d 895 (1985) )—civil forfeiture actions were successful in obtaining two sums of United States currency alleged to be the proceeds of narcotics transactions. The alleged purpose of the SONAL account at Miami's Capital Bank, opened in 1980 by a Colombian money exchanger and travel agent, Beno Ghitis, was to receive deposits of American dollars from persons who wished to sell the dollars to Ghitis' agency in return for checks drawn on the SONAL account and/or pesos to be delivered by Ghitis' agency in Colombia. Approximately one week after the account was opened, the bank began receiving cash deposits ranging from $500,000 to $1 million in small denomination bills. When informed that the bank's holding company refused to insure any cash in the bank over $1 million, Ghitis negotiated with the bank president, who allowed the deposits to continue after Ghitis agreed to pay one-half of one percent of the funds deposited monthly as a service fee. After that agreement, a Ghitis partner began depositing $1 million to $2 million in the account two or three times a week. The bank's fee would presumably have brought monthly income in the range of $40,000 to $120,000 from this one account.

After one of Ghitis' partners became concerned with the large amounts of cash, despite Ghitis' assurance that it was not derived from drug trafficking, the partner approached United States Customs officials, who investigated the SONAL account. When they were convinced that the evidence demonstrated probable cause that a substantial connection existed between the cash and drug trafficking, more than $3 million in cash and more than $4 million in the bank account were seized (and later forfeited to the government). Subsequent inspection of SONAL's records showed that between January 1, 1981 and August 21, 1981—a period of less than eight months—deposits of cash to the SONAL account totalled more than $242 million.

## BANK SECRECY ACT

With the enactment of the Bank Secrecy Act in 1970, Congress attempted to legislate banking policies to disrupt laundering. The Bank Secrecy Act provides that banking institutions must file a Currency Transaction Report (CTR) for each deposit, withdrawal, or exchange of more than $10,000. The law also requires that a Currency or Monetary Instruments Report (CMIR) be filed with the U.S. Customs Office if more than $5,000 in cash leaves the United States. Finally, the law mandates that a person declare ownership of foreign financial accounts on his or her federal income tax return.

Initially, enforcement of the law was delayed for five years while questions of its constitutionality were settled. Additional delay was caused by uncertainty over which agencies would be responsible for insuring compliance. Among the other problems that have hindered the detection and prosecution of money launderers—some of them addressed in subsequent amendments to the law—have been the banks' lack of emphasis on validating the identity of individuals making currency transactions; low compliance rates with CTR requirements among some financial institutions; and long delays in entering CTRs into Treasury Department computers (U.S. General Accounting Office, 1981; U.S. Senate, 1983).

Recommendations of the Kaufman Commission to remedy shortcomings in the Bank Secrecy Act include voluntary guidelines to encourage: training of bank personnel in detection of suspicious transactions; increased internal audit capabilities among banks so as to facilitate Bank Secrecy Act compliance; on-site electronic data processing of Bank Secrecy Act reporting forms; and formal bank policies that direct bank employees to report suspicious transactions to authorities.

One of the commission's administrative recommendations has already been adopted: Legal casinos have been classified as "financial institutions" by the U.S. Treasury Department under the provisions of the Bank Secrecy Act, a measure intended to reduce the use of casinos as conduits for money laundering. Other administrative recommendations include: appointing federal agency contacts to work with financial institutions in achieving compliance with the Bank Secrecy Act; consolidating the processing of CTR data in a single location; and allocating additional FBI and U.S. Drug Enforcement Administration personnel to money laundering investigations.

This attention to banks indicates a subtle shift between earlier commissions and the Kaufman Commission: the emphasis turned toward those legitimate institutions and actors that facilitate organized criminality.

However, the banking industry has expressed concern about the federal government's incursion into the privacy of banking transaction records. Representative is a statement by Hjalma Johnson, President of the Florida Banking Association, who commented: "We have to be careful about enacting new laws that might go after a small percentage of dishonest people, and then trample on the privacy rights of a lot of innocent people" (*New York Times*, November 6, 1984). As an alternative to increased governmental intrusion, the bankers' association is attempting to educate its members about prevention of money laundering, and Operation Greenback officials are pleased with bankers' increased awareness of laundering (interviews with federal prosecutors, 1984).

Nevertheless, despite signs of improved bank cooperation, New England's largest bank recently pleaded guilty to shipping unreported cash to foreign banks (*Time*, February 25, 1985), as have banks in California and elsewhere. More indictments may be on the horizon, and case law is developing in response to attempts to circumvent the reporting requirements of the Bank Secrecy Act through multi-transaction laundering or "smurfing" (*U.S. v. Puerto*, 1984; *U.S. v. Tobon Bailes*, 1983; *U.S. v. Sans*, 1984). (However, the ninth federal circuit recently joined the first circuit in refusing to consider "structured" laundering transactions involving under $10,000 as violations of the Bank Secrecy Act.) Banking officials who sought a promise of amnesty from the federal government for reporting their earlier failure to file currency transfer information have been met with reluctance by Treasury Department officials (Ricks, 1985).

The next five years will no doubt be crucial in determining the effectiveness of the Bank Secrecy Act and prosecution efforts such as Miami's Operation Greenback. Some of the remedies are administrative, and can be carried out if federal agencies will allocate sufficient resources and cooperate among themselves. Other solutions are more tenuous, since they prescribe aggressive self-policing by financial institutions.

## CONCLUSION

The forms of criminality analyzed in the Kaufman Commission's money laundering report represent a major shift away from more traditional crimes, particularly those relying on "muscle." Surely no one would seriously assert that organized criminal interests have "penetrated," "infiltrated," or otherwise taken over the legitimate banking industry in south Florida, Los Angeles, Houston, New York, or elsewhere. "Penetration" and "infiltration" may be wholly appropriate descriptions of organized criminals' entry into key mozzarella cheese distributorships or into the toxic waste disposal industry and pornographic bookstores, but such terms are not useful for understanding how criminality may be facilitated by major legitimate societal institutions. Rather, the laundering issue typifies the possibilities for criminal capital to enjoy many of the advantages of licit capital through use of institutions ill-equipped and relatively unmotivated to hamper such laundering efforts. Further development of these lines of inquiry by the Kaufman Commission, such as by targetting of lawyers and other professionals who exceed the bounds of the legitimate client relationship, may prove to be fruitful.

Further analysis by the Kaufman Commission of the financial aspects of narcotics trafficking and organized criminality should focus on the utility of several innovative statutes and methods of investigation and prosecution of organized criminals. The use of criminal and civil RICO, the Continuing Criminal Enterprise statute, and various civil asset forfeiture statutes has grown in recent years. Perhaps the interest of the Kaufman Commission in financial crime will strengthen those striving to develop strong case law on laundering.

Because organized crime has changed as dramatically as the legitimate American economy in the years since the 1967 presidential organized crime commission report, it is inevitable that new criminal methods and opportunities have proliferated. As legitimate capital has been "internalized," so too has illegitimate capital. What is important is that the Kaufman Commission, despite its concomitant interest in traditional facets of organized criminality, has emphasized several enduring and vital issues: the interaction of the illegitimate sector with the legitimate sector; the increasingly difficult task of separating criminal capital from legitimate capital; and the equally difficult task of detecting and prosecuting the movement of criminal capital.

## References

Bell, Daniel (1962). "Crime as an American Way of Life: A Queer Ladder of Social Mobility." In *The End of Ideology*, edited by Daniel Bell. New York: Collier Books.

Blau, Charles W., *et al.* (1983). *Investigation and Prosecution of Illegal Money Laundering: A Guide to the Bank Secrecy Act*. Washington, DC: U.S. Department of Justice, Criminal Division.

Cressey, Donald R. (1969). *Theft of the Nation: The Structure and Operations of Organized Crime in America*. New York: Harper Colophon Books.

Interviews with federal prosecutors (1984). Miami, FL.

Karchmer, Clifford L. (1985). "Money Laundering and the Organized Underworld." In *The Politics and Economics of Organized Crime*, edited by Herbert Alexander and Gerald E. Caiden. Lexington, MA: Lexington Books.

Kefauver, Estes (1951). *Crime in America*. Garden City, NY: Doubleday.

Kennedy, Robert F. (1960). *The Enemy Within*. New York: Harper and Row.

Lernoux, Penny (1984). *In Banks We Trust*. Garden City, NY: Anchor Press/Doubleday.

McClellan, John L. (1962). *Crime Without Punishment*. New York: Duell, Sloan and Pierce.

Meeker, James W. and John Dombrink (1984). "Criminal RICO and Organized Crime: An Analysis of Appellate Litigation." *Criminal Bulletin* 20 (4):309–320.

Moore, William Howard (1974). *The Kefauver Committee and the Politics of Crime, 1950–1952*. Columbia, MO: University of Missouri Press.

*New York Times* (1984). November 6.

Ricks, Thomas E. (1983). "Joel Hirschhorn Says Defending Smuggler Helps Cause of Justice." *Wall Street Journal*, June 27.

Schelling, Thomas C. (1967). "Economic Analysis of Organized Crime." Appendix D, *Task Force Report: Organized Crime*. U.S. President's Commission on Law Enforcement and Administration of Justice, Task Force on Organized Crime. Washington, DC: U.S. Government Printing Office.

*Time* (1985). February 25.

U.S. General Accounting Office (1981). *Bank Secrecy Reporting Requirements Have Not Yet Met Expectations, Suggesting Need for Amendment*. Washington, DC.

U.S. National Commission on Law Observance and Enforcement (Wickersham Commission) (1968). *Reports* (1930–1931). Reprint. Montclair, NJ: Patterson Smith.

U.S. President's Commission on Law Enforcement and Administration of Justice (1967). *Task Force Report: Organized Crime*. Washington, DC: U.S. Government Printing Office.

U.S. President's Commission on Organized Crime (1984). *The Cash Connection: Organized Crime, Financial Institutions and Money Laundering*. Interim Report to the President and the Attorney General. Washington, DC: U.S. Government Printing Office.

U.S. Senate (1958). *Select Committee on Improper Activities in the Labor or Management Field*. Interim Report (March 24).

_____ (1983). Permanent Subcommittee on Investigations. *Crime Secrecy: The Use of Offshore Banks and Companies*. Staff Study by the Permanent Subcommittee on Investigations of the Committee on Government Affairs. 98th Congress, First Session.

*U.S. v. $4,255,000*, etc., *et al.*, and U.S. v. $3,686,000, etc., *et al.*, 762 F. 2d 895 (1985).

*U.S. v. Puerto*, 730 F. 2d 627 (1984).

*U.S. v. Sans*, 731 F. 2d 1521 (1984).

*U.S. v. Tobon-Bailes*, 706 F. 2d 1092 (1983).

# Tilting at Windmills: The Chicago Crime Commission v. Organized Crime, 1980–1984

*Dennis E. Hoffman*

*A case study is presented of the Chicago Crime Commission's response to organized crime in Chicago from 1980–1984. Commission activities intended to combat organized crime are described, using information obtained from interviews with the executive director of the commission, commission position papers, internal organizational records, and the testimony of commission representatives before a U.S. Senate subcommittee. An interpretation is offered as to why certain anti-organized crime activities were successful and others unsuccessful.*

The purposes of this paper are to describe the Chicago Crime Commission's response to organized crime from 1980–1984 and to interpret the outcomes of the commission's chosen strategies. It should be emphasized that this is a modest beginning in an area where little research has been done. No systematic study has ever been conducted on private sector efforts directed against organized crime. And previous studies of citizen participation in crime prevention (e.g., Washnis, 1976; Pennell, 1979; Podolefsky and DuBow, 1981) failed to examine either the role of the economic elite or citizens' crime commissions in efforts directed against organized crime.

## THE CHICAGO CRIME COMMISSION

Formed in 1919 by the Chicago Association of Commerce, the Chicago Crime Commission is the oldest, most active, and most respected citizens' crime commission in the United States. Influential businessmen and civic leaders established the organization to prevent crime and to wage war against corruption and inefficiency within the criminal justice system. This elite group had a rather significant impact upon the Chicago Police Department, but only in those areas that coincided with law enforcement interests, such as increasing police manpower and administrative efficiency (Haller, 1971).

The commission's national reputation stems from its publicity campaign against organized crime in the 1930s. Concerned about the openly illicit activities of top gangsters in Chicago, the commission sought to mobilize the community and criminal justice officials to take action. The commission published the first "public enemies list," which was printed by the Chicago newspapers. The list named Al Capone as "Public Enemy Number One," a term which thereafter became part of the public lexicon (Goldberg, 1940).

Organized crime is still a major focus of the commission in the 1980s. Today, however, the commission also conducts performance evaluations of felony court judges, collects and disseminates information on gangs to police and prosecutors, operates a "Report Crime in Your Neighborhood" program offering a 24-hour anonymous tip hotline, and carries out a variety of other anti-crime programs (Chicago Crime Commission, 1984a).

To a large extent, the commission and its activities are a reflection of its executive director. The executive director manages the affairs of the commission, takes the lead in formulating commission goals, oversees program development and operations, maintains liaison with criminal justice agencies, and serves as the organization's main lobbyist before city, county, state, and federal legislative bodies (Healy, 1985c).

Patrick F. Healy has been the executive director since 1980. Mr. Healy's professional background in criminal justice includes four years as an Assistant State's Attorney for Cook County, Illinois, three years as an Assistant U.S. Attorney for the Northern District of Illinois (which encompasses Chicaco), and 14 years as the Executive Director of the National District Attorneys Association (Healy, 1985c).

The executive director is appointed by a board of directors. The approximately 60 men and women on the board come from the top echelon of the business community. Formally, the board is supposed to establish the policies, programs, and procedures of the commission (Chicago Crime Commission, 1982b). Informally, the executive director, acting with the consent of the board, is responsible for most policy initiatives and positions on issues.

An executive committee, made up of the president, vice presidents, the treasurer, the immediate past president, and several members of the board of directors, is vested with the same powers and duties as the board. The president is the most important officer. The president presides at meetings of the executive committee, the board of directors, and the full commission. Equally important, the president and the executive director are the only authorized spokespersons for the commission.

The general membership consists of about 380 prominent Chicago business leaders. Members vote in commission elections and also sit on committees relating to areas such as the police, courts, corrections, legislative matters, and the inner city.

## Function and Resources

"Watchdog" is the term most befitting the commission's function. This organization monitors the behavior of government officials responsible for law enforcement. When the commission detects what it considers to be a flawed practice in an agency, or determines that a change is necessary in the criminal law, commission representatives first utilize a work-behind-the-scenes strategy. They privately negotiate with an agency, trying to effect change through persuasion. If this fails, the commission goes to the media to generate public pressure.

A key to the commission's attempts to influence criminal justice policy is its use of its members as resources: members contribute their names, money, and manpower. Much of the potential power of the commission as a pressure group rests with the "quality" or status of the members. Thirty-three of the 48 persons on the commission's board of directors in 1984 were chairmen, presidents, or vice-presidents of corporations. Most of the other directors are senior partners or partners in prestigious law and accounting firms (Chicago Crime Commission, 1984a). Having an elite membership provides the commission with easy access to elected officials, agency heads, and other criminal justice decision-makers.

Money given by members, as well as other concerned individual, foundation, and corporate donors, makes the commission's work possible. The "donor honor roll" reads like a list of the "Fortune 500." The Allstate Foundation, the Amoco Foundation, Arthur Anderson and Company, the First National Bank of Chicago, Illinois Bell Telephone, Kraft, Inc., and Sears and Roebuck were among the companies donating $5,000 or more in 1984 (Chicago Crime Commission, 1984a).

Members of the commission also provide specific skills, expertise, and equipment. Senior partners in law firms, for example, are instrumental in evaluations of judicial conduct and performance.

## Politics

The politics of the Chicago Crime Commission must be inferred from its programs and activities, since the commission's constitution and bylaws mandate non-partisanship. Officers of the commission cannot publicly endorse or participate in the election campaign of candidates for any public office directly related to the administration of justice. Also, the commission excludes from membership public officials, candidates for public office, law enforcement officers and others in the criminal justice system, and news media representatives (Chicago Crime Commission, 1982b). These restrictions are intended to ensure that the commission acts on behalf of the public interest and, in the process, avoids conflicts of interest and a loss of objectivity.

Despite these safeguards, the commission's positions on criminal justice issues have been politically conservative. A punitive orientation has been a recurring theme throughout the commission's history. During its early years, the commission supported the death penalty, criticized the courts for allowing criminals to escape conviction due to plea bargaining, and sought to restrict the use of probation and parole (Haller, 1971). In the early 1980s, the commission advocated crackdowns on the "victimless" crimes of prostitution and gambling, called for more severe punishment of armed robbers, and criticized judges for allowing unnecessary delays in the processing of court cases (Chicago Crime Commission, 1984a).

## ANTI-ORGANIZED CRIME APPROACHES
## AND ACTIVITIES

The following analysis of the commission's activities to control organized crime is based on Podolefsky and DuBow's (1981) typology of citizen-based, collective responses to crime. A "social problems approach" deals indirectly with crime; it attacks conditions that are seen as the root causes of crime. This approach reflects the view that crime is intertwined with other social problems. The "victimization prevention approach," on the other hand, attempts to reduce opportunities for victimization. Three subcategories comprise the victimization prevention approach: (a) protective behavior aims at reducing the likelihood of victimization of oneself, one's household, one's business, or other members of the community; (b) criminal justice-oriented approaches use the criminal law and criminal justice agencies to detect crime and punish criminals; and, (c) surveillance approaches involve patrol or watching of certain areas or groups such as gangs.

## Promoting Community Awareness:
## Example of the Criminal Justice Approach

If citizens are to become involved in any crime prevention or control program, they must be made aware of the crime problem and opportunities for participation (National Crime Prevention Institute, 1978). The Chicago Crime Commission has continually engaged in consciousness-raising activities on the subject of organized crime since 1919. Public enemies lists, biographical sketches of syndicate leaders and their crimes, and other types of information are continually released to the media and thus provided to the public.

A special campaign was carried out in 1983 to heighten the public's awareness of organized crime and to provide a basis for the passage of a commission-sponsored, anti-organized crime legislative package. At a U.S. Senate Subcommittee on Investigations' field hearing in Chicago on March 4, 1983, testimony on the topic of "Organized Crime in Chicago" allowed the Chicago Crime Commission to communicate its view of the problem and the solutions.

Media coverage of the hearing was extensive. The *Chicago Tribune* "hyped" the event in news articles a month before the senators came to Chicago (*Chicago Tribune*, February 16, 1983). In part, media interest stemmed from the slaying of mob figure Allen Dorfman in Chicago in January 1983, and a bungled assassination attempt against gambling entrepreneur Ken Eto in Chicago a month later.

The hearing itself was dominated by the commission. Four of the eight persons who testified were affiliated with the commission: Robert G. Blakey, Professor of Law, Notre Dame University, and co-drafter of some of the commission's anti-organized crime bills; Patrick Healy, executive director of the commission; Gail Melick, then president of the commission and Executive Vice-President of the Continental Illinois National Bank and Trust Company of Chicago; and William F. Roemer, Jr., consultant to the commission and former special agent of the Federal Bureau of Investigation.

Melick, the banker, stressed the economic costs of organized crime, including tax money expended on criminal justice, consumer dollars spent on higher costs of goods and services, and jobs lost to workers because businesses prefer not to locate in a city where organized crime is prevalent (U.S. Senate, 1983).

Executive director Healy offered the subcommittee this economic solution:

> We should use more fines and confiscation of assets. The name of the game for organized crime is money. Take their money away,

they are going to lose interest . . . We must strip them of their ill-gotten gains (U.S. Senate, 1983:13).

This was a reference to the Racketeer Influenced and Corrupt Organizations (RICO) provisions, which, according to Healy afforded an opportunity to attack the profits of organized crime.

Blakey, the law professor, elaborated on Healy's proposed solution. He pinpointed the civil sanctions of RICO as a way of getting at the property, money, and power of organized crime. He also strongly endorsed the commission's legislative package, which included a state RICO bill. Blakey asserted that Illinois law failed to provide law enforcement authorities with the tools necessary to deal with organized crime:

> [Illinois] has no statewide grand jury, it has no use immunity provision, it has no electronic surveillance, it does not have a modern theft and fencing statute, and it does not have a RICO statute—until the State of Illinois and similar major industrial states arm their law enforcement people with this kind of legislation, you will not have the kind of impact on organized crime, not only at the Federal level, but also at the State and local level, that our people are entitled to expect from their government [U.S. Senate, 1983:77].

Not coincidentally, the commission's anti-organized crime bills (to be discussed in the next section) provided (with the exception of a statewide grand jury) what Blakey charged was lacking in Illinois law.

The testimony of Roemer, the former FBI agent, presented the standard FBI image of organized crime. An organizational chart of the top leadership and soldiers in La Cosa Nostra was displayed to show the structure of organized crime in Chicago. Roemer also offered recollections from his days as a special agent about ties between Chicago politicians and organized crime.

Also testifying were the Special Agent in Charge of the Chicago Division of the FBI, the Special Agent in Charge of the Chicago Field Division of the Drug Enforcement Administration, the Special Agent in Charge of the Chicago Organized Crime and Racketeering Section of the Department of Labor, and the Superintendent of the Chicago Police Department. Consensus existed between the testimony of the federal authorities and the commission's witnesses on the following points: (1) An alien criminal conspiracy, namely La Cosa Nostra, is behind organized crime; (2) The Chicago family of La Cosa Nostra is hierarchically structured and is operated by certain key persons; and, (3) Effective investigative tools have aided in the prosecution of organized criminals at the federal level and should be instituted at the state and local level by the Illinois State Legislature.

Since the purpose of the testimony given by commission representatives was to lay the groundwork for passage of its bills, the impact of the hearing can be assessed by looking into the fate of the commission's legislative package.

## Lobbying for an Anti-Organized Crime Legislative Package: An Example of the Criminal Justice and Surveillance Approaches

The commission launched a major legislative initiative against organized crime at the state level in 1983. Four bills were designed to provide effective tools for law enforcement officials: (1) a Racketeer Influenced and Corrupt Organizations Act (RICO); (2) a Theft, Fencing, and Related Offenses Control Act; (3) a Use Immunity Act; and, (4) an Eavesdropping Control Act. Three of the four bills were derived from federal legislation. The commission's RICO and use immunity bills were based on Title IX of the Organized Crime Control Act of 1970, while the electronic surveillance bill was based on Title III of the Omnibus Crime Control and Safe Streets Act of 1968.

The commission's version of RICO would have prohibited operating, acquiring, or investing in any enterprise, public or private, characterized by a pattern of racketeering. "Enterprise" was defined to include licit associations (e.g., corporations, labor unions, and governmental units) as well as illicit associations (e.g., gambling, narcotics, and prostitution). This new racketeering offense would have been a Class I felony under Illinois state law, with penalties including imprisonment and fines. The proposed act also provided for an alternative fine of three times the loss or gain from criminal activity. A provision of the bill allowed for the criminal forfeiture of unlawful transactions and bases of power. The bill also would have authorized public and private civil suits for injunctive relief from racketeering, and provided for victims of racketeering to recover treble damages (Healy and Blakey, 1983).

Implicit in the commission's support for RICO was an economic explanation of organized crime. The commission perceived organized crime to be a serious threat to the free enterprise system. RICO was intended to deter organized criminals from involvement with legitimate business by taking the profit out of racketeering; if convicted under RICO, an offender may have to return profits to the victims of the crime. Additionally, RICO was intended to allow victims to recover the costs of investigation, prosecutions, and losses due to fraud (Healy and Blakey, 1983).

The Theft, Fencing, and Related Offenses Act would have created a new crime of "dealing in stolen property." Aimed at "chop shop" practitioners, this proposal would have imposed higher criminal penalties for fencing, and made it easier to prove that criminals are dealing in stolen auto parts (Chicago Crime Commission, 1983).

A third piece of legislation would have provided for use immunity in prosecuting white collar and organized crime. This bill would have permitted prosecutors, legislative committees, and administrative committees to grant immunity from the use of testimony or any information derived from such testimony. The goal was to encourage witnesses to testify in organized crime cases (Chicago Crime Commission, 1983).

The fourth proposed law, the Eavesdropping Control Act, would have expanded the use of electronic surveillance (Chicago Crime Commission, 1983). According to the commission, Illinois law is too restrictive in requiring that one party consent to a wiretap, and also that a wiretap be monitored by both the court and the state's attorney's office. Under the commission's proposed law, the one-party consent rule would have been dropped, and electronic surveillance by law enforcement agencies could have occurred with the approval of a state's attorney and a specifically designated court (Cook County State's Attorney's Office, 1985).

To secure passage of the bills, the commission held public hearings in Chicago in 1983. After the hearings, the commission submitted the bills to the Illinois state legislature. Political parties in both houses sponsored the legislation. Patrick Healy made numerous trips to Springfield to lobby on behalf of the proposed laws, while the American Civil Liberties Union lobbied against all of the bills.

Three of the four bills passed the Senate, but the electronic eavesdropping bill never got out of the Illinois Senate subcommittee. The commission's explanation of the defeat of this bill is that politicians had an interest in opposing an expanded eavesdropping law that might be used against them in political corruption cases. James Zagel, the Director of the Illinois Department of Law Enforcement and the Chairman of the Governor's Advisory Council on Criminal Justice Legislation, concurred with the commission's view:

> Electronic eavesdropping, I think is the most difficult thing to pass in this state. It is facing some major difficulties. The first is that the Illinois General Assembly was on two occasions, itself a subject of eavesdropping. Once they had a lobbyist that taped some conversation of the State House and was a subject of litigation in 1968. And on another occasion a State Senator was sent and wired by the federal government in an investigation of corruption in the Illinois

General Assembly. That has caused incredibly bad feelings despite the fact that what occurred then would occur again within the law today because it was a federal investigation [Zagel, 1984:86].

The RICO, Anti-Theft, and Immunity bills were sent to the House Rules Committee, where all died. The RICO bill was the most controversial. Executives of some large corporations and accounting firms in Chicago, despite sitting on the Chicago Crime Commission's Board of Directors, were instrumental in the bill's defeat. Lobbyists for these business interests argued that the Senate-passed measure was overly broad and could be used in civil suits against people with no connection to organized crime (*Chicago Tribune*, June 11, 1984). Equally important, the commission's own lobbying efforts were stymied by the failure of its board members to support the bills through testimony before the Rules Committee and through personal contacts with legislators (anonymous Illinois state senator, 1985).

## Opposition to the Extension of Legalized Gambling: An Example of the Criminal Justice Approach

Some types of gambling have been legal in Illinois since 1927, when the legislature approved pari-mutuel betting. Bingo for charities was legalized in 1971, and the Illinois lottery came into existence in 1974. And in 1980, charitable raffles and jar games were declared by the legislature to be legal on a local option basis.

The Chicago Crime Commission opposed every attempt to extend legalized gambling in the State of Illinois from 1980–1984. Casino gambling was the commission's first target. The commission opposed casino gambling when a proposal was made to develop a hotel-casino complex in Chicago in 1982. Legalizing casino gambling, according to the commission, would result in the following problems: (1) diversion of money away from legitimate business and away from the state lottery and pari-mutuel betting; (2) an increase in street crimes such as auto theft, robbery, rape, and prostitution; (3) organized crime domination of casino gambling; (4) the use of casinos for laundering money obtained through drug trafficking and other illegal means; (5) the growth of the loansharking business because of gamblers' need for ready cash in large amounts; (6) increases in the rates of social forms of deviance, such as suicide and alcoholism; (7) increases in law enforcement costs because of higher crime; and (8) a general decline in the quality of life, making new business wary about locating in Chicago and families leery about raising children in the city (Chicago Crime Commission, 1982a).

Casino gambling was not legalized in 1982. Moreover, whenever the issue has resurfaced, as it has several times since then, the commission has staunchly opposed it, and efforts on behalf of legalization have failed.

The commission's most recent anti-gambling activities centered around a 1985 bill to legalize off-track betting (OTB). After Governor James R. Thompson's task force on Illinois horse racing recommended OTB as a means of producing $22 million annually for state and local governments, the commission mounted a counterattack. A barrage of press releases, letters to the editor, and a widely circulated position paper on OTB were issued by the commission.

The state's United Methodist Church joined the commission, passing a resolution that opposed all legalized gambling. (Two members of the Chicago Crime Commission's Board of Directors drafted part of that resolution.) Several community organizations formed a coalition with the commission against OTB, while State's Attorney Richard M. Daley and Sheriff Richard Elrod also went on record as opposing the bill.

Nevertheless, the Illinois Senate approved the measure 31–26. The commission stepped up its attack on the bill once it was in the House. Joel D. Gingiss, president of the commission and head of Gingiss International, Inc., testified against the proposed bill. Gingiss, along with Patrick Healy and commission board members William G. Stratton (a former governor of Illinois and presently Vice-President of the Chicago Bank of Commerce), and Samuel Witwer (past president of the Illinois Constitutional Convention and a partner in Witwer, Moran, Burlage, and Witwer), met privately with Governor Thompson to present their case (Chicago Crime Commission, 1985a).

The commission asserted that OTB would not raise enough money to be an effective public financing tool and that government-supported OTB was intended primarily to subsidize the horse racing industry instead of allowing free competition for the entertainment dollar (Chicago Crime Commission, 1985b). Mob-controlled illegal bookmaking, in the commission's view, would flourish under OTB because of better odds, unlimited credit lines, and confidentiality from the Internal Revenue Service. The commission also posited that legalized off-track betting would provide bookies with a place to direct their unprofitable bets. Finally, the commission contended that OTB would cause increases in the number of compulsive gamblers, especially among the poor (Chicago Crime Commission, 1985b).

When members of the House voted 94–2 (with 21 voting "present") to cease discussions, the bill died on June 25, 1985. The commission's own explanation of the outcome acknowledges that in-fighting between the supporters of dog and horse racing was partially responsible for the bill's defeat (Healy, 1985a). At a minimum, however, it would seem that the commission's leadership of the opposition was a contributing factor to the bill's demise.

## Name Checks:
## An Example of Protective Behavior
## or the Criminal Justice Approach?

The commission's "Business Advisory Name Check Service" provides legitimate businesses with information about criminal connections of a potential loan applicant, employee, client, vendor, or business (Chicago Crime Commission, 1981). The officially stated purpose of this activity is to help companies ascertain whether the persons they are doing business with have any organized crime ties (Healy, 1985a). Data gathered for this service come from a variety of sources, including newspaper clippings, court records, books, pamphlets, and speeches. Since 1980, the commission has averaged 3,000 to 5,000 requests for information each year. Table 1 provides a breakdown of inquiries for information by type of organization for the first six months of 1984.

### Table 1
Requests for Information by Different Types of Organizations
for January, 1984–June, 1984*

|  | N | % |
|---|---|---|
| Banks/Savings & Loans Assoc. | 126 | 6.41 |
| Business | 66 | 3.36 |
| Credit Agencies | 38 | 1.94 |
| Federal Agencies | 12 | .61 |
| Insurance Companies | 20 | 1.01 |
| Investigative Agencies | 612 | 31.15 |
| Law Enforcement Agencies | 261 | 13.28 |
| Law Firms | 14 | .72 |
| Media | 100 | 5.08 |
| Police Departments | 345 | 17.55 |
| Public Inquiry | 51 | 2.60 |
| Real Estate | 4 | .20 |
| Sheriff's Office | 164 | 8.35 |
| Miscellaneous | 152 | 7.74 |
|  | 1965 | 100.00 |

*Source: Chicago Crime Commission, 1984b.

What is most striking about Table 1 is that the types of organizations making the most frequent use of name checks are *not* businesses. Although the formal objective of name checks is to provide a service to the business community, the top four users of the service are investigative agencies, police departments, other law enforcement agencies, and the Cook County Sheriff's Office. Together these criminal justice related organizations accounted for over 70 percent of all requests.

That private security firms should be among the main beneficiaries of a program set up for and funded by the private sector seems appropriate. However, the finding that municipal police departments and county sheriffs' offices also are clients suggests a reversal of roles, with crime information being collected by the commission (a private entity) and flowing to public law enforcement agencies.

Table 2 presents the same information by geographic location of the party making the request.

**Table 2**
Geographic Origin of Requests for Information*

|              | N    | %      |
| ------------ | ---- | ------ |
| City         | 746  | 37.97  |
| Suburbs      | 419  | 21.32  |
| Out-of-State | 800  | 40.71  |
|              | 1965 | 100.00 |

*Source: Chicago Crime Commission, 1984b.

A rather anomalous finding is the large number of out-of-state requests. According to the executive director (Healy, 1985b), most of the out-of-state requests come from private companies seeking information on individuals with addresses or business activities in Chicago.

In 1985 the commission began to cut back this service because of a lack of resources necessary to adhere to federal rules about checking the accuracy of references and other statements (Healy, 1985b).

This service can be regarded as a mixture of criminal justice and protective approaches. Despite the formal goal of the Business Advisory Name Check Service, the actual operations of the program suggest that it is also partially geared to assist public law enforcement agencies.

## OBSERVATIONS ON OUTCOMES AND IMPACTS

Why were certain of the commission's anti-organized crime activities successful and others unsuccessful? The defeat of the commission's legislative package is partly attributable to the self-interested reaction of some politicians who wanted to avoid the possibility that their own or their colleagues' deviant behavior would be exposed. Such a self-serving response was at odds with the commission's public interest objective of providing law enforcement authorities with more effective tools to use against organized crime as well as forms of white collar crime such as political bribery.

On a more philosophical level, the conflict between due process and crime control values played a role in determining the fate of the four bills. The American Civil Liberties Union stressed in its lobbying efforts that electronic surveillance, use immunity, and the other proposed bills were potentially threatening to the civil liberties of American citizens. By contrast, the commission, which adhered to a crime control perspective, argued that the civil liberties trade-offs associated with the use of certain investigative and prosecutorial instruments were necessary because organized crime itself poses a threat to civil liberty—a threat that cannot be effectively met without the deployment of weapons that might compromise civil liberties.

The commission's scaling down of the name check operation demonstrates this conflict between civil liberties and organized crime control. A fear of lawsuits tightened the lips of commission spokespersons regarding the organized crime ties of individuals. Specifically, the commission reduced its business advisory service because it could not comply with federal guidelines and court decisions pertaining to libel, slander, and other related areas. A few years earlier the commission was sued for $3 million by a Chicago man for alleged defamatory statements contained in pamphlets published by the organization. Though dismissed by a trial court, the Appellate Court of Illinois reversed the dismissal of the libel suit and ordered the trial body to reconsider the plaintiff's claim that the commission's alleged defamations had interfered with his business (*Colucci v. Chicago Crime Commission*, 1975).

What would have happened if successful outcomes had occurred for all of the commission's activities? Some conclusions and suggestions are offered for those who would look to investigative and prosecutorial tools, name checks, and the criminalization of gambling as strategies to reduce organized crime activity.

First, the prosecution of organized crime leaders does little to eliminate organized crime. Electronic surveillance, use immunity, and other tools (with the exception of RICO) are mainly useful in developing cases against key organized crime figures. As the history of enforcement efforts against organized crime indicates, demands still remain for illicit goods and services after leaders are incapacitated; opportunists in criminal groups merely take the place of those locked up.

Second, name checks may have some utility for reducing organized crime's infiltration into legitimate business. Yet the overall impact may be limited since the few objective research studies on the subject indicate that organized criminal intrusions into legal business are "a phenomenon of small and declining importance" (Reuter, Rubinstein, and Wynn, 1983:14; see also Reuter, 1983).

Third, while experience with organized crime control gives federal law enforcement authorities confidence in the efficacy of the tools advocated by the commission, more is needed as a basis for organized crime policy. Albanese (1985) pointed out that objective empirical evidence is lacking on the costs versus benefits of use immunity. Regarding federal electronic surveillance law, Albanese cites evidence showing that wiretapping is expensive, invasive of individual privacy, and unproductive since only about one-half of all wiretaps result in convictions.

Fourth, RICO is a potentially powerful weapon against organized crime. The thrust of RICO is that criminal syndicates must be dealt with as organizations, not as individuals. Such an organizational approach is alien to the individual bias of the criminal law. Yet organizations and their profits are the relevant targets in many situations involving organized crime. Thus, research is needed into why more extensive use is not made of RICO. Meeker and Dombrink (1984), in a study of federal appeals court decisions on RICO litigation, reached these important conclusions: (1) Claims (such as those made by the dissenting members of the commission) that RICO is used to single out nonracketeers, or often used creatively against other white collar offenders, are unfounded; and (2) Federal prosecutors do not employ the asset forfeiture provisions of RICO very frequently because they are mainly concerned with convictions and because extra effort is required on the part of prosecutors to litigate issues of asset forfeiture.

Fifth, citizens' public interest organizations as well as government officials, should give more thorough consideration to the value of social problems approaches to organized crime control. Such an approach would attempt to eliminate *opportunities* for organized crime. Empirical research by Albini (1971), Anderson (1979), Smith (1980), Abadinsky (1981), Luksetick and White (1982), and Albanese (1984), indicates that the legalization or regulation of particular types of illicit behavior may curb organized crime. For example, Marcum and Rowen's (1974) evaluation of legalized gambling raises doubts about the efficacy of reducing organized crime through the criminalization of gambling. They assert that if a community wants to rid itself of illegal gambling operators, then it will legalize gambling and impose low taxes on it so that it can compete with illegal gambling. Marcum and Rowen suggest an alternative to the American or Las Vegas model of legalized gambling. Under the "British Model," gambling is viewed as a social problem rather than as a source of revenue.

## CONCLUSION

A fair conclusion to be drawn from this study is that the Chicago Crime Commission served basically as an extension of the official justice system. In its participation in the U.S. Senate Subcommittee on Investigations hearing, the commission played the role of "promoter of the official definition of organized crime." In its sponsorship of the anti-organized crime bills, the commission assumed the role of "stalking horse." Law enforcement officials, though strongly supportive of the proposed legislation, remained in the background and allowed the commission, as a public interest organization, to front the bills. In its name check service, the commission played the role of "information gatherer" for both private and public police. And finally, in its opposition to legalized gambling, the commission played the role of "protector of public morality." From the commission's view, gambling could be designated as a "crime" since it involves various wrongs that people do to themselves, others, and the community as a whole. Based on the consequences of these wrongs, such as increases in the number of compulsive gamblers and a decline in the quality of life, the commission justified its notion of gambling as a crime.

Turning to the efficacy of the commission's response to organized crime, two observations can be made. First, the commission's attempt to combat organized crime was thwarted by forces inside the commission as well as by forces in the political-economic environment. But organizational-strategic problems that impaired the commission's effectiveness, such as the lack of sustained lobbying by board members for the organized crime bills, posed less of an obstacle than barriers in the external environment, such as civil liberty concerns or the self-interests of politicians.

Second, activities of the commission did not deviate markedly from traditional criminal justice system tactics. The problem is that the criminal justice system's response to organized crime has not been proven especially effective. The commission's experience demonstrates that private sector activites need to be more resourceful in developing effective strategies against organized crime.

## References

Abadinsky, H. (1981). *The Mafia in America: An Oral History.* New York: Praeger.

Albanese, J.S. (1984). *Justice, Privacy, and Crime Control.* Lanham, MD: University Press of America.

_____ (1985). *Organized Crime in America.* Cincinnati, OH: Anderson Publishing Co.

Albini, J.L. (1971). *The American Mafia: Genesis of a Legend.* New York: Irvington.

Anderson, A.G. (1979). *The Business of Organized Crime.* Stanford, CA: Hoover Institution Press.

Anonymous Illinois State Senator (1985). Personal interview. Chicago.

Chicago Crime Commission (1981). *Ignoring Crime Is Criminal.* Chicago: Chicago Crime Commission.

_____ (1982a). "Casino Gambling." Press Release (January 19).

_____ (1982b). "Constitution and By-Laws." *How to Organize and Operate a Citizens Crime Commission.* Chicago: Chicago Crime Commission.

_____ (1983). "Public Hearings for Pending Organized Crime Legislation." *Searchlight* (October):6–7.

_____ (1984a). *Annual Report.* Chicago: Chicago Crime Commission.

_____ (1984b). "Name Checks Records." Chicago Crime Commission's Internal Files.

_____ (1985a). "Lottery to Lose Millions to OTB." Press Release (June 17).

_____ (1985b). "Off-Track Betting is a Bad Bet." Position Paper.

*Chicago Tribune* (1983). "Big Drive is Readied Against Mob." (February 16):4.

_____ (1984). "Far Reaching Crime Bill Comes Up Short" (June 11):28.

*Colucci v. Chicago Crime Commission* (1975), 34 N.E. 2d. 461 (Ill. App.).

Cook County State's Attorney's Office (1985). "Illinois Wiretap Laws Most Restrictive in Nation." *State's Attorney's News* 5 (2):1.

Goldberg, W.A. (1940). *The Chicago Crime Commission.* Ph.D dissertation, Department of Sociology, Northwestern University.

Haller, M. (1971). "Civic Reformers and Police Leadership: Chicago, 1905–1935." In: *Police in Urban Society*, edited by H. Hahn. Beverly Hills: Sage.

Healy, P.F. (1985a). Personal Interview. Chicago (June 24).

_____ (1985b). Telephone Interview. Chicago (October 22).

_____ (1985c). Vita. Personnel Files of the Chicago Crime Commission.

Healy, P.F. and G.R. Blakey (1983). "Debate Continues Over Proposed Illinois RICO." *Chicago Daily Law Bulletin* 14:5.

Luksetick, W.A. and M.D. White (1982). *Crime and Public Policy: An Economic Approach*. Boston: Little, Brown.

Marcum, J. and H. Rowen (1974). "How Many Games In Town?" *Public Interest* 36 (Summer):25–52.

Meeker, J. and J. Dombrink (1984). "Criminal RICO and Organized Crime: An Analysis of Appellate Litigation." *Criminal Law Bulletin* 20 (4):309–320.

National Crime Prevention Institute (1978). *Understanding Crime Prevention*. Lexington, KY: National Crime Prevention Institute Press.

Pennell, F.E. (1979). "Private vs. Collective Strategies for Dealing With Crime, Citizen Attitudes Toward Crime and the Police in Urban Neighborhoods." *Journal of Voluntary Action Research* 7:1–2, 59–75.

Podolefsky, A. and F. DuBow (1981). *Strategies for Community Crime Prevention*. Springfield, IL: Charles C. Thomas.

Reuter, P. (1983). *Disorganized Crime: The Economics of the Visible Hand*. Cambridge, MA: MIT Press.

Reuter, P., J. Rubinstein, and S. Wynn (1983). *Racketeering in Legitimate Industries: Two Case Studies*. Washington, DC: U.S. National Institute of Justice.

Smith, D.C. (1980). "Paragons, Pariahs, and Pirates: A Spectrum-Based Theory of Enterprise." *Crime & Delinquency* 26 (July):358–386.

U.S. Senate. Permanent Subcommittee on Investigations (1983). "Organized Crime in Chicago." Washington, DC: U.S. Government Printing Office.

Washnis, G. (1976). *Citizen Involvement in Crime Prevention*. Lexington, MA: Lexington Books.

Zagel, J. (1984). "Overcoming Obstacles at State and Municipal Levels: Some Needed Legislative Tools." In: *Organized Crime In Chicago: Myth and Reality*, edited by T.M. Frost and M. Seng. Chicago: Loyola University.

# Part IV:
# Organized Crime
# Involvement in
# Legitimate Business

# Predicting the Incidence of Organized Crime: A Preliminary Model*

## Jay S. Albanese

*The empirical literature on organized crime has greatly expanded in the last 15 years. Much of that literature is primarily descriptive, and does little to explain the genesis and growth of organized crime activity. This paper reports on an exploratory attempt to predict "high risk" business conditions that can lead to the infiltration of legitimate business by organized criminals. Using the results of recent theoretical and empirical investigations, a preliminary predictive model is proposed that serves as a starting point for a more rational allocation of law enforcement resources in anticipating and reducing the likelihood of organized crime infiltration into legitimate business.*

### PREDICTING THE INCIDENCE OF ORGANIZED CRIME

The last 15 years have witnessed incredible growth in the quality of empirical research on organized crime. Beginning with Joseph Albini's pioneering work (1971), and continuing with the research of Ianni and Reuss-Ianni (1973), Smith (1975), Anderson (1979), Nelli (1981), and Reuter (1983), among others, there has been an increase in both the quality and volume of empirical investigations of organized crime (see Albanese, 1985).

Much of this work grew from a dissatisfaction with traditional notions of organized crime promulgated by the U.S. government and widely accepted by the public. The Kefauver hearings in 1950, Valachi hear-

---

*An earlier version of this paper was presented at the Annual Meeting of the Academy of Criminal Justice Sciences, Las Vegas, March 1985.

ings in 1963, and the President's Crime Commission in 1967 served both to establish and perpetuate the popular belief that the bulk of organized crime in North America is controlled by a nationwide conspiracy dominated by Italian-Americans. This characterization of organized crime has found no support among objective investigators of the problem, although the notion of a national criminal conspiracy remains popular among government agencies and the general public. Clearly, the results of recent empirical investigations have not been widely read or believed by most Americans. It is for this reason that organized crime research continues to emphasize descriptions of the precise nature and characteristics of organized crime (see Albanese, 1983; Peterson, 1983). The persistence of this popular belief in a national "Mafia" or "Cosa Nostra" has kept many researchers from pursuing more explanatory, rather than descriptive, accounts of organized crime.

In other areas of criminal justice research, such as juvenile delinquency or the effects of incarceration, descriptive accounts were superseded long ago by attempts to explain the nature, incidence, and reasons for the problem (see Goffman, 1961; Sutherland, 1939). Such a point in the development of the literature on organized crime has been reached only by a handful of investigators. It is time that research in this area concentrated on empirical rather than anecdotal attempts to demystify the organization of organized crime.

## The Nature of Prediction

It is widely held that prediction is the fundamental aim of all science (Gottfredson, 1967; Albanese, 1984). Whether we are attempting to explain cancer, crime, or drug use, a common objective in all investigations is to be able to predict the occurrence of the behavior. Such an ability to predict certain outcomes enables the investigator to understand the situational factors that cause a condition, its correlates, and possible ways in which to alter those conditions to eliminate the problem. In many areas of the natural and social sciences, the ability to predict undesirable behaviors or conditions, such as disease or parole violations, also makes public policy decisions and daily management decisions more rational.

## The Utility of Prediction to Law Enforcement

Law enforcement agencies have been granted many powerful investigative and prosecution tools during the last 20 years, including the use of wiretap evidence in court, use-immunity of witnesses to gather evidence, special grand juries, the witness protection program, and the Racketeer

Influenced and Corrupt Organizations Act (RICO) special prosecution provisions. Evaluations of organized crime prosecutions, however, have not shown overwhelming success. Independent evaluations of the prosecutions of the Federal Organized Crime Strike Forces, state and county rackets bureaus, labor racketeering prosecutions, and gambling prosecutions in 17 different cities have found "no agreement on what organized crime is," "no consensus" on the activity to be targeted, "a variety" of jurisdictional problems, the "same schemes . . . and the same suspects" that have dominated the field for 20 years, and "no system of accountability" (see Blakey, Goldstock and Rogovin, 1978; Fowler, Mangione and Pratter, 1978; Stewart, 1980; U.S. Comptroller General, 1977, 1981).

A problem noted in each of these evaluations of organized crime prosecutions has been the lack of focus and direction. There appears to be a continuing problem of who to investigate, in what manner, for how long, and to what purpose. Unlike traditional police work, where law enforcement agencies react to complaints and calls for service, organized crime investigations must be proactive. Victims of organized crime rarely call the police for help because they are subject to duress, extortion, or cooptation. As a result, police usually must begin an investigation to determine if a crime has been committed at all.

Proactive investigations often lead to dead-ends, since no investigator, no matter how experienced, can keep abreast of all the schemes and other dealings being developed by organized crime elements. As a consequence, organized crime investigations often result in a great deal of wasted time and unnecessary expenditure of resources. Therefore, many law enforcement agencies do not take the time to develop serious or complex cases, and choose instead to arrest the careless or flagrant gambler, drug dealer, or prostitute as the opportunity arises. Clearly, such an approach does nothing to reduce the incidence of the more serious forms of organized crime.

If the conditions that give rise to the infiltration of organized crime into legitimate businesses could be predicted, however, law enforcement agencies could realize major benefits. Resources would not be wasted on fruitless investigations, manpower could be allocated more rationally according to which industries are predicted to be especially vulnerable, and the long-range interests of the community would be better served by a concentration on truly serious organized misbehavior.

## Efficiency of Predictive Models

Any predictive model endeavors to show a relationship between certain independent (predictor) variables and a dependent variable (the criterion to be predicted). In criminological applications, the pioneering work in this area was done by Gottfredson, Wilkins, and Hoffman (1978) in their efforts to develop a more rational method to determine who should be released on parole and which sentences are best suited for certain offenders. Their research found that two variables best account for parole board and judicial sentencing decisions: the seriousness of the offense and the prior record of the offender. This finding has been replicated in many other studies, most of which have involved the prediction of success on probation or parole (see Albanese, Fiore, Powell, and Storti, 1981; Gottfredson and Gottfredson, 1980; Monahan, 1981).

The good news is that criminological prediction models thus far have proved to be fairly simple and practical. Currently, some states are using parole and sentencing guidelines that are based on prediction models. Similar applications of these models could be introduced by other agencies. The bad news is that their predictive efficiency, or accuracy, has been low. The best models that attempt to predict success of probationers or parolees have generally predicted 20 to 30 percent of the outcomes correctly; the remainder are "misses" or incorrect predictions, which involve certain costs of their own (see Wilkins, 1980). Nevertheless, an inefficient prediction model can be a very useful screening device, as will be shown later.

The predictive model proposed here is different from earlier work in criminological prediction, which has primarily involved the prediction of the future behavior of *individuals* based on the performance of similar individuals in the past. The model described here attempts to predict *business conditions* that render a business vulnerable to organized crime infiltration, based on the experiences of similar businesses in the past. Therefore, this organized crime model is predicting an intermediate condition (i.e., high-risk businesses), rather than the ultimate behavior of concern (organized crime). This model, then, does not attempt to predict organized crime per se, but seeks to predict conditions within a business that are conducive to organized crime infiltration.[1]

It is assumed that different types of businesses may well have different probabilities of organized crime infiltration depending upon the nature of the business, its complexity, the manner in which it conducts business, and the history of the industry. As a result, the model offered here deals solely with businesses in general. It will remain for subsequent investigations to gather empirical evidence to determine whether different models are required to predict high-risk conditions in various industries.

**Prior Work**

There has been very little empirical research on organized crime infiltration of legitimate business. An early case study was conducted by Edward

De Franco (1973) of a planned bankruptcy by organized criminals. Another, more recent investigation by Reuter, Rubinstein, and Wynn (1983) examined organized crime infiltration of the solid waste collection and vending machine industries.

Theoretical work also has been limited. Serious consideration of modeling organized crime began with Thomas Schelling's (1967) economic analysis of organized crime for the President's Crime Commission. Although he argued that organized crime tends to deal in markets with inelastic demand (which has found support in later empirical studies), he also believed that organized crime generally was present in large-scale operations that attempted to obtain monopoly control over a particular market. The available empirical literature does not appear to support this conclusion, however (see Reuter, 1983; Reuter, Rubinstein and Wynn, 1983).

In 1971, Joseph Albini found that an important factor in both business and personal relationships involving organized crime was "patronage." Obviously, in certain markets there are individuals in positions of power and influence ("patrons"), who can help others ("clients") requiring their assistance. A "patron-client" relationship forms as a natural consequence of these conditions. For example, in certain businesses it may be difficult to obtain a license or loan, or to attract customers. If a financially or politically influential "patron" can assist in overcoming these problems, a patron-client relationship is formed. Now, the client owes his patron money or favors, which may result in a wide variety of illicit activities such as loansharking, political "favors," or extortion. This relationship can become extended throughout a business or market when the client later acts as a patron for someone with less power and influence. The result is the emergence of "powerful syndicate figures who serve as patrons to their functionaries [and who] may also serve as clients to others more powerful than they" (Albini, 1971:265). It is reasonable to hypothesize, therefore, that poorly trained owners or managers, who are ill-equipped to deal with business problems, are more likely to become targets (potential "clients") for organized crime infiltration than are professional, well-trained, and well-equipped operators.

Perhaps the most detailed effort to model organized crime was attempted by Dwight Smith. His organized crime model evolved through several publications, culminating in 1980 with his "spectrum-based theory of enterprise" (Smith, 1975; 1978; 1980). Borrowing from general organization theory, Smith hypothesized that organized crime develops in the same manner as legitimate business. That is, it responds to the "task environment" of a market, consisting of customers, suppliers, regulators, and competitors. Like legitimate business, organized crime attempts to survive and make a profit, while dealing with the pressures of its task environment. Several authors have made limited efforts to further refine and apply Smith's model (see Martin, 1981; Dintino and Martens, 1981).

## A PRELIMINARY PREDICTIVE MODEL

Extrapolating from Smith's and Albini's explanations, it would appear that certain types of business conditions (i.e., configurations of customers, suppliers, regulators, competitors, and patron–client relationships) would be more conducive to organized crime infiltration than others. For example, De Franco's (1973) study of a planned bankruptcy found that it began with a large bank deposit to establish credit for a struggling wholesale meat business. No notice was given to the firm's suppliers, customers, or regulators that a "new" management was now in place. Large orders were then placed, using the bank deposit as credit. After the orders were received, they were converted into cash through a fence or surplus property dealer. The company was then forced into bankruptcy by its creditors when no payment was forthcoming. The result is a business that has been milked of all of its assets through a scam. De Franco concluded that businesses and banks should be aware of signals that might indicate a scam. These signals include: a large deposit used for a credit reference elsewhere, an unusual amount of credit inquiries, new business management with only vague information about the principals, and "rush" requests for deliveries not corresponding to normal patterns.

Applying the principles of Smith's theory of enterprise, it can be seen from De Franco's study that certain elements of the meat business's task environment were ripe for infiltration. Entry into the wholesale meat business was easy (little regulation), the demand for meat was fairly constant (guaranteed customers), the market in the area was favorable (customers and suppliers would not readily move to other competitors because product and costs are similar throughout the market), and there was a need for capital (supply). As Albini might suggest, a "new" management disseminating "vague" information about the principals may also indicate infiltration resulting from an illicit patron–client relationship. In this way, specific market conditions may help to predict the incidence of organized crime infiltration of legitimate business.

Reuter, Rubinstein, and Wynn's (1983) investigation of the solid waste collection industry in the New York City area provides another case study for this preliminary model. In their investigation of private firms that collected commercial waste, they found conditions similar to those identified in the wholesale meat business example: It was easy for individuals to enter the market (little regulation), the industry was populated by numerous "small, frequently family-based, enterprises," with little difference in service among vendors (open competition in a market of non-professional managers), there was inelastic demand for the service (customers always available), and many firms were identified with "minimal capital and no reserve equipment" (supply for illicit patrons). Clearly, market conditions appear similar in both the bankruptcy scam and solid waste infiltration case studies.

Table 1 summarizes the preliminary predictive model described here. The first four predictors are taken from Smith's model, the fifth from Albini's notion of "patron–client" relationships, while the sixth (prior history) is taken from previous research in criminological prediction that has found prior record to be predictive of criminal behavior (see Simon, 1971; Gottfredson, Wilkins, and Hoffman, 1978).

**Table 1**
Predicting Organized Crime Infiltration
into Legitimate Business

| *Predictors* | *Low Risk* | *High Risk* |
|---|---|---|
| Supply | Few available small, financially weak businesses | Readily available small, finacially weak businesses |
| Customers | Elastic demand for product | Inelastic demand for product |
| Regulators | Difficult to enter market | Easy to enter market |
| Competitors | Monopoly/oligopoly controlled market | Open market with many small firms |
| Patronage | Entreprencurs are professional managers | Entrepreneurs are non-professionals ill-equipped to deal with business problems |
| Prior record | No prior record of organized crime involvement in market. | Prior history of organized crime infiltration in industry. |

## Limitations

The preliminary prediction model described in this paper is clearly not the last word in organized crime prediction. It is likely to require refinement in several important areas, most of which result from problems inherent in all prediction research. First, the model may be "overfitted" to the available empirical research. As shown, there have been very few empirical investigations of organized crime infiltration into legitimate business. The two case studies described in the previous section may not be typical and, therefore, the model may be fitted to non-representative cases or industries. Additional case studies are clearly necessary to determine whether this model can be generalized to other industries.

Similarly, the model assumes that all industries have the same predictive attributes. Like other research in criminological prediction, what holds true for one sample may not hold true for others (see Wright, Clear, and Dickson, 1984). It is possible that different models may be required for different industries. Additional case studies of organized crime infiltration in various industries will indicate whether other variables must be considered for efficient prediction models in different types of markets.

Third, a "base rate" problem may hamper the design of a prediction model; the proportion of businesses that have problems with organized crime infiltration may be too small to develop an efficient prediction model. Simply stated, the more uncommon an event, the more difficult it is to predict accurately. The base rate for various industries can only be determined through further empirical research.

Finally, the measurement of such variables as "supply," "competitors," and the other predictors shown in the model can be difficult. Factors such as "financial condition," "types of supplier," and "competitive conditions," are nominal or, at best, ordinal measures of a business situation. Therefore, the ordering of these variables involves some creativity on the part of the investigator. Future work should examine carefully the measurement units employed in scaling predictive factors to guard against the masking of any true predictive relationship based on inappropriate counting or measurement units.

## CONCLUSION

In spite of the limitations noted in the preceding section, there is reason to believe that the prediction model proposed here may form the foundation for a more useful approach to the investigation of organized crime. First, criminological prediction models have been found, generally, to have a limited number of important predictor variables. In fact, Gottfredson and Gottfredson (1980) maintain that little predictive accuracy is gained by the inclusion of large numbers of variables in a prediction model. Therefore, a six-variable model does not necessarily oversimplify the situation.

Second, the prediction model does not necessarily have to predict business conditions conducive to organized crime infiltration with a high degree of accuracy to be useful. For example, probation and parole prediction devices have found models with relatively low predictive efficiency to be useful in distinguishing "high risk" groups of offenders from "low risk" groups. In this way, supervision or release decisions can be based on something more rational than "unguided discretion" (see Gottfredson, Wilkins and Hoffman, 1978; Albanese, Fiore, Powell and Storti, 1981). Likewise, the classification of high-risk and low-risk markets may be useful to investigators of organized crime, even if precise prediction of organized crime activity within individual businesses is not possible. An analog to this procedure has already been attempted in case-screening techniques developed for use by police. The Rochester, N.Y. Police Department developed a system called "Early Case Closure," in which information was gathered to assess the "solvability" of robberies and burglaries. By directing their resources toward crimes with the best chance of solution (and by spending *less* time on cases with little chance of solution), the department was able to significantly improve its clearance rates for those crimes (see Bloch and Bell, 1976). A similar effort was undertaken by the Stanford Research Institute and the Police Executive Research Forum. They developed a model for screening burglary cases, based on factors associated with the crime. Applying the system retrospectively, they were able to predict whether a burglary case would be solved 85 percent of the time (cited in Walker, 1983). In a similar way, law enforcement officials can reduce the amount of time spent on dead-end organized crime investigations with the use of the prediction model proposed here. A law enforcement agency could use such a model as a screening device in its jurisdiction. Investigative resources could be focused on those markets identified as "high-risk" for infiltration, and perhaps less time would be wasted on investigations that do not lead to prosecution.

Finally, the true value of a model to predict the infiltration of legitimate businesses by organized crime will not be realized until additional empirical investigations are conducted in different types of businesses. It has long been held, for instance, that organized crime has infiltrated certain businesses in the pizza, fish and meat, linen supply, and trucking industries. These might be useful starting points for the application and refinement of a model to predict the incidence of organized crime in other industries.

## Notes

1. It has been argued elsewhere that organized crime can be grouped into three types: (1) provision of illicit goods; (2) provision of illicit ser-

vices; and (3) the infiltration of legitimate business. The first two types involve the marketing of illicit drugs, gambling, financing, or sex. In each of these cases, the offender and the victim voluntarily engage in a mutual exchange of goods or services. On the other hand, the infiltration of legitimate business by means of extortion is a predatory crime; there is a clear offender and victim. This type of crime, then, will be the subject of the predictive model proposed in this paper.

## References

Albanese, Jay S., Bernadette A. Fiore, Jerie H. Powell and Janet R. Storti (1981). *Is Probation Working?: A Guide for Managers and Methodologists.* Washington, DC: University Press of America.

Albanese, Jay S. (1983). "God & the Mafia Revisited: From Valachi to Fratianno." In: *Career Criminals*, edited by G. Waldo. Beverly Hills: Sage.

_____ (1984). *Justice, Privacy, and Crime Control.* Lanham, MD: University Press of America.

_____ (1985). *Organized Crime in America.* Cincinnati: Anderson.

Albini, Joseph L. (1971). *The American Mafia: Genesis of a Legend.* New York: Irvington.

Anderson, Annelise G. (1979). *The Business of Organized Crime.* Stanford, CA: Hoover Institution Press.

Blakey, G. Robert, Ronald Goldstock and Charles H. Rogovin (1978). *Rackets Bureaus: Investigation and Prosecution of Organized Crime.* Washington, DC: U.S. Government Printing Office.

Bloch, Peter B. and James Bell (1976). *Managing Investigations: The Rochester System.* Washington, DC: Police Foundation.

De Franco, Edward J. (1973). *Anatomy of a Scam: A Case Study of a Planned Bankruptcy by Organized Crime.* Washington, DC: U.S. Government Printing Office.

Dintino, Justin J. and Frederick T. Martens (1981). "The Process of Elimination: Understanding Organized Crime Violence." *Federal Probation Quarterly* 45 (June):26–31.

Fowler, Floyd J., Thomas W. Mangione and Frederick E. Pratter (1978). *Gambling Law Enforcement in Major American Cities.* Washington, DC: U.S. Government Printing Office.

Goffman, Erving (1961). *Asylums.* Garden City, NY: Anchor Books.

Gottfredson, Don M. (1967). "Assessment and Prediction Methods in Crime and Delinquency." In: *President's Commission on Law Enforcement and Administration of Justice. Task Force Report: Juvenile Delinquency and Youth Crime.* Washington, DC: U.S. Government Printing Office.

Gottfredson, Don M., Leslie T. Wilkins and Peter B. Hoffman (1978). *Guidelines for Parole and Sentencing: A Policy Control Method.* Lexington, MA: Lexington Books

Gottfredson, Michael R. and Don M. Gottfredson (1980). *Decisionmaking in Criminal Justice: Toward a Rational Exercise of Discretion.* Cambridge, MA: Ballinger.

Ianni, Francis A.J. and Elizabeth Reuss-Ianni (1973). *A Family Business: Kinship and Social Control in Organized Crime.* New York: New American Library.

Martin, W. Allen (1981). "Toward Specifying a Spectrum-Based Theory of Enterprise." *Criminal Justice Review* 6 (Spring):54–57.

Monahan, John (1981). *Predicting Violent Behavior: An Assessment of Clinical Techniques.* Beverly Hills: Sage.

Nelli, Humbert S. (1981). *The Business of Crime: Italians and Syndicate Crime in the United States.* Chicago: University of Chicago Press.

Peterson, Virgil W. (1983). *The Mob: 200 Years of Organized Crime in New York.* Ottawa, IL: Green Hill Publishing.

Reuter, Peter (1983). *Disorganized Crime: The Economics of the Visible Hand.* Cambridge, MA: MIT Press.

Reuter, Peter, Jonathan Rubinstein and Simon Wynn (1983). *Racketeering in Legitimate Industries: Two Case Studies.* Washington, DC: U.S. National Institute of Justice.

Schelling, Thomas C. (1967). "Economic Analysis and Organized Crime." In: *President's Commission on Law Enforcement and Administration of Justice, Task Force Report: Organized Crime.* Washington, DC: U.S. Government Printing Office.

Simon, Frances (1971). *Prediction Methods in Criminology.* London: Her Majesty's Stationery Office.

Smith, Dwight C. (1975). *The Mafia Mystique.* New York: Basic Books.

––––– (1978). "Organized Crime and Entrepreneurship." *International Journal of Criminology and Penology* 6:161–177.

––––– (1980). "Paragons, Pariahs, and Pirates: A Spectrum-Based Theory of Enterprise." *Crime & Delinquency* 26 (July):358–386.

Stewart, Robert C. (1980). *Identification and Investigation of Organized Crime Activity.* Houston, TX: National College of District Attorneys.

Sutherland, Edwin (1939). *Principles of Criminology.* Philadelphia: Lippincott.

U.S. Comptroller General (1977). *War on Organized Crime Faltering: Federal Strike Forces Not Getting the Job Done.* Washington, DC: U.S. General Accounting office.

––––– (1981). *Stronger Federal Effort Needed in Fight Against Organized Crime.* Washington, DC: U.S. General Accounting Office.

Walker, Samuel (1983). *The Police in America.* New York: McGraw-Hill.

Wilkins, Leslie T. (1980). "Problems with Existing Prediction Studies and Future Research Needs." *Journal of Criminal Law and Criminology* 71 (Summer):98–101.

Wright, Kevin N., Todd R. Clear and Paul Dickson (1984). "Universal Applicability of Probation Risk-Assessment Instruments: A Critique." *Criminology* 22 (February):113–134.

# America's Toxic Waste Racket: Dimensions of the Environmental Crisis

## Frank R. Scarpitti
## and Alan A. Block

*In recent years organized crime in the U.S. has extended its tradi-tional activity in solid waste hauling to include the disposal of toxic wastes. This new service provided by organized crime around the country coincided not only with a substantial increase in the amount of waste produced, but also with the passage of state and federal legislation making disposal cumbersome and expensive. Evading the legislation enabled illegal haulers and disposal site operators to earn huge profits. More importantly, when waste haulers tied to organized crime moved into the business of toxic waste disposal, they brought with them "business as usual" atti-tudes and practices with potentially long-term, detrimental conse-quences for significant portions of the population. Because state regulatory and enforcement agencies are ill-equipped to control such practices, additional responsibility must be assumed by the U.S. Environmental Protection Agency (EPA). For political and philosophic reasons, however, that agency has done little to con-trol the problem of illegal toxic waste disposal.*

The poisoning of America by the illegal and indiscriminate disposal of toxic and hazardous waste is a problem of enormous magnitude. Indus-trial poisons are seeping their way into the food chain and the drinking water supply in ways that make it unlikely, if not impossible, to stop. Among the many reasons this happens is that organized crime is involved in the illegal and dangerous disposal of the most deadly wastes known to humans (U.S. House of Representatives, 1981b).

115

Organized crime is not the only culprit involved in this extraordinarily dangerous development. Responsibility for the situation also rests with many waste haulers and disposers not affiliated with syndicated crime, as well as with numerous generators of toxic wastes. Some of the largest and most prestigious companies in the petro-chemical industry deal with "midnight dumpers" or organized crime disposal firms because they provide a cheap way of getting rid of their most harmful wastes (Brown, 1981; Krajick, 1981; McKenna, 1983). Government, too, has failed to protect the public welfare. The laws passed to regulate the toxic and hazardous waste disposal industry have enough loopholes in them to allow the biggest tankers through. And, if that is not enough encouragement for illegal dumpers, the almost total lack of meaningful enforcement is.

To understand the current problem and its origin, we must begin by examining the history of garbage collection and disposal in the United States. Since the nineteenth century, American law has recognized the right of government to exercise police power in control of certain types of enterprises that affect the public interest (McCraw, 1975). Thus, as Charles Reich points out, government creates "new property" in many areas by granting licenses and permits that allow holders to do business, but under the controls of the state. In order to supervise its largess, government achieves new rights "to investigate, to regulate, and to punish" (Reich, 1964:746). Regulatory agencies are allowed a wide range of discretion and possess powerful sanctions, including withdrawal of the right to do business. In addition, misuse of government permission to operate firms may even be defined as criminal. In all cases, though, the theoretical goal of the agency is to regulate the profit-motivated activity of permit holders so as to ensure that the public interest is being served.

Among the many businesses controlled by state licenses and permits is the solid waste industry (Savas, 1977:170–182), including private garbage haulers, and owners and operators of landfills, dump sites, and incinerators. Supervision and control of this industry through licensing has been in place in most states for at least two decades.

The obvious relationship between public health and garbage collection and disposal has made trash a highly profitable business enterprise for haulers and dump site owners (Reuter, n.d.). The profitability of the waste disposal business also has contributed to its infiltration by organized crime. Around the country, particularly in the populous northeast, garbage collection and disposal have fallen increasingly into the hands of organized crime figures. Beginning in 1957 with the U.S. Senate's McClellan Committee hearings, and continuing through more recent federal and state investigations, the ability of racketeers to structure the garbage collection industry has been established (U.S. Senate, 1957). Commenting on the 1957 McClellan hearings, Peter Reuter observes:

> It is clear from all of this that by the time the Committee began its investigations, racketeers had control of the industry. The union was responsive to their demands and the carters made little effort to resist. Racketeers had direct and indirect interest in numerous companies [Reuter, n.d.:64].

As the McClellan hearings documented organized crime's control of waste disposal in greater New York and Los Angeles, state legislative committees did the same for New Jersey in 1959 and 1969 (New Jersey Senate, 1959; New Jersey Special Legislative Commission, 1969). In both instances, a web of relationships existed among organized crime figures, local teamsters' officials, corrupt politicians, and waste haulers. In the 1970s, several prosecutions again established the influence of the Gambino and Genovese groups in the New York industry (Reuter, n.d.). With the help of a U.S. Federal Bureau of Investigation (FBI) informant, New Jersey officials indicted some 50 individuals and companies in 1980 for waste racketeering (New Jersey Superior Court, 1980b). And, in February 1985, a number of New York organized crime figures, including the alleged "godfathers" of the city, were indicted for the illegal control of waste hauling, among other charges (New York State Supreme Court, County of Suffolk, 1984).

Organized crime's illegal waste-related activities have not changed over the decades. Owners are organized into trade associations that dictate the local rules of the game, while workers are controlled by union officials. Territory is parceled out and becomes the sole property of one hauler, thereby eliminating competition and customer choice. Bids are rigged and cash payments are skimmed. As one might expect, the controlling mobsters' rules are enforced through violence (Goldstock, 1985).

Although the actual extent to which organized crime controls and dominates the waste disposal business is unknown, it is clear that organized crime figures have been actively involved in this industry. In more recent years, official and public interest have shifted to the disposal of toxic wastes (Shabecoff, 1983). Recent estimates by the U.S. Environmental Protection Agency (EPA) indicate that 150 million metric tons of toxics were generated in the U.S. in 1981; 10 *billion* pounds annually in New Jersey alone, according to another recent estimate (Wilheim, 1981). The EPA estimates that only a small percentage of toxics are disposed of properly (Brown, 1980). In addition, estimates of the number of dump sites used for industrial poisons range up to 120,000 (Krajick, 1981).

## RCRA AND THE EPA

In order to protect society from improper and illegal dumping of toxic wastes, Congress enacted the Resource Conservation and Recovery Act (RCRA) in October 1976. The objective of this act was to establish a minimum set of standards and regulations for the control of hazardous wastes that would be applicable throughout the nation. States were free to adopt more stringent standards, but in their absence the EPA would enforce the RCRA standards and guidelines.

The act envisioned the control of toxic wastes by a system of manifests designed to track the waste from the generator, through the carting agent, to its final disposal site. Through this technique, the present location and ultimate destination of identified wastes can be known and monitored. Regulation is enhanced by a permit system requiring waste generators, transporters, treaters, storers, or dump operators to obtain authorizations for their operations. Each operator qualifies for a permit by meeting standards specified in the act or in accompanying regulations developed by the EPA. Although RCRA establishes a federal system of permit-granting and regulation enforcement, it allows transfer of these responsibilities to the state if the state enacts laws at least as strict as the RCRA. Transporters are required to obtain an identification number from the EPA, haul only waste accompanied by a signed manifest, and transport their cargo to known and licensed facilities. Operators of disposal facilities must sign the manifest and return it to the generator within 30 days, noting any discrepancy between the manifest and what is actually deposited at their sites. At the same time, performance standards enforced by the EPA govern the manifest systems, treatment, storage and disposal of waste, and the location of disposal sites.

The statute has placed the primary focus of reform on waste *disposal* rather than waste generation. Instead of inhibiting production or demanding new technology that might control waste production, the system of permits, licenses, manifests, inspections and, ultimately, "good faith" compliance by waste generators, may well have compounded and complicated waste regulation. Unscrupulous or uncaring generators may cope with their need to dispose of toxic wastes by assigning all such activity to dumpers whose methods of disposal they do not question or probe (U.S. District Court, District of New Jersey, 1981). In addition, a system based on licenses and inspections is susceptible to corruption of various sorts, and might serve more to facilitate the illegal exchange of money than to attack the problem at hand.

The structural deficiencies of RCRA have been magnified by the history of its implementation since 1976. From the time of its passage, this law has been something of an EPA stepchild, languishing in unfulfilled promises, never being permitted to reach its admittedly limited potential. Many observers have been highly critical of EPA for long delays in identifying hazardous wastes and their characteristics, as well as its delay in creating and issuing new standards (Brown, 1981). Not only did this lackadaisical approach permit the dumping of toxics to continue virtually uncontrolled, it also inhibited the enactment of regulatory statutes in many states. Not knowing what the federal regulations might be, most states simply waited until federal action was taken so as not to be in conflict with EPA standards.

Ironically, federal and state legislation created to impede illegal dumping may actually be encouraging it by raising the cost of compliance. The profit motive appears to be quite prominent in the decision of how to dispose of generated toxics. Chemical neutralization or burial in sealed, ecologically safe areas is expensive, costing perhaps hundreds of dollars per 55-gallon drum. Faced with seemingly excessive costs to dispose of their wastes in a non-hazardous manner, some generators apparently accept the services of illegal haulers and site operators whose fees, although high, are more acceptable (New York State Senate, 1980; U.S. House of Representatives, 1982; McKenna, 1983). Illegal disposal by "midnight dumpers" of great sophistication and guile represents a relatively inexpensive alternative, thus keeping the costs of production competitively low. By not complying with federal and state regulations, illegal haulers and site operators are capable of earning huge profits. Under these conditions, it is not surprising to find that organized crime figures have now become involved in every aspect of the hazardous waste disposal industry.

## ORGANIZED CRIME AND HAZARDOUS WASTE

As the need to dispose of hazardous wastes became more acute in the 1970s, the great demand for services and the concomitant potential for profits created new carting opportunities for solid waste haulers. By handling hazardous chemical wastes as well, these carters created a "new" industry, one that is highly corrupt, rife with organized crime connections, and exceedingly violent. The outline of this problem has been stated by Congressman John D. Dingell of the House Subcommittee on Oversight and Investigations:

> It is appalling enough when disposers of hazardous waste, through inadvertence or ignorance, recklessly poison the environment and endanger the public health. But it is considerably more disturbing

when generators, haulers, and disposers—in order to avoid the cost
of legitimate disposal—engage in the practice of illicit dumping for
profit. In the course of the inquiries of the subcommittee, we have
developed information linking organized crime to the illegal dumping of toxic wastes. This comes as no surprise. In fact, it was predictable, given the lucrative nature of this activity [U.S. House of
Representatives, 1981b].

Evidence substantiating organized crime's involvement in toxic
waste disposal can be found in the reports and files of state and federal
investigating committees, state and local police agencies, grand jury indictments and trial transcripts, and articles of incorporation of waste
companies. In addition, former illegal dumpers have testified to various
law enforcement agencies about the role of organized crime figures and
syndicates in this industry. On the basis of available evidence, it appears
reasonable to conclude that known organized crime figures play a prominent role in the hazardous waste industry, particularly in the industrial
states of the northeast and midwest, despite attempts to regulate the industry by enforcing various codes and standards (U.S. House of Representatives, 1980; 1981b; New York State Senate, 1980). While a number
of such figures own waste disposal companies and dump sites, either
directly or indirectly, others serve as officers of such companies or
related enterprises. In addition to illegally dumping hazardous wastes
into landfills, sewers, rivers, on farms and elsewhere, companies controlled by organized crime figures forge manifests, mislabel containers,
rig bids, engage in restraint of trade, and corrupt state agents charged
with safeguarding the public welfare (McKenna, 1983; Hinchey, 1984;
Block and Scarpitti, 1985).

Examples of organized crime's involvement in the hazardous waste
disposal industry are numerous. One of the first public statements about
this relationship occurred in testimony before the New York State Senate
Select Committee on Crime in the summer of 1980. John H. Fine, who
headed the New York Metropolitan Region Office of the State Organized
Crime Task Force, noted some of the organized crime figures and their
often bewildering series of companies involved in the hazardous waste
industry. In the fall of 1977, Fine became aware that "the Rockland
County Sheriff's Patrol with help from town police and tips from a local
radio reporter had begun an investigation into the take-over of the
Ramapo town landfill by certain organized crime elements." The Organized Crime Task Force moved in to participate in the investigation,
which was only one of several investigations "into organized crime's
take-over of landfills, toxic waste hauling concerns, and racketeer infil-

tration of ostensibly legitimate business in the toxic and solid waste area" (New York State Senate, 1980:474, 502).

Fine's investigation led from Rockland County to New York City, especially Staten Island, and more specifically the towns along the Arthur Kill, the body of water separating Staten Island from New Jersey. Fine stated that "we discovered in Orange County [New York] that a landfill authorized to take only solid non-toxic waste was the site of dumping of hazardous waste materials" by reputed organized crime firms (New York State Senate, 1980:528). Additionally, tank trucks from New Jersey were using the site, indicating that the manifests filed in New Jersey by the waste haulers were fraudulent, as were the corresponding records filed with the New York Department of Environmental Conservation, which merely registered a post office box as the destination of hundreds of thousands of gallons of toxic waste.

During the late 1970s and early 1980s, a great deal more was learned about organized crime and toxic waste, especially in the northeast. Investigations have revealed that the major New York City and New Jersey syndicates are directly involved in the toxic waste disposal business in this region (Block, 1983; McKenna, 1983). This is especially true of the Genovese/Tieri crime syndicate. Also prominent, though, are members and associates of the Gambino, Bonanno, Lucchese, and De Cavalcante organizations. Not only do they own and operate hauling firms and landfills, but they have moved into related areas, with costly and sometimes deadly results.

The operation of waste disposal or treatment plants is an example of organized crime's penetration of this industry. One such plant in Elizabeth, New Jersey was taken over by a reputed organized crime figure at gunpoint. Tens of thousands of drums of waste were allegedly stockpiled on the grounds of the plant, which was located in a heavily populated area. When the entire facility was engulfed by a fire of suspicious origin, toxic fumes threatened the health of residents in both New Jersey and New York (New York State Senate, 1980). At a treatment facility operated by alleged organized crime affiliates in Perth Amboy, New Jersey, "Fortune 500" companies sent their waste to be incinerated. Unfortunately, according to an indictment, the plant had no incinerator, and was instead flushing the waste into the city sewer system and a nearby waterway (New Jersey Superior Court, 1980a).

Available information has pointed up the national involvement of organized crime in the toxic waste business. From New York to New Mexico, from New Jersey to Florida, a pattern of waste racketeering may be observed (Block and Scarpitti, 1985). In fact, a recent survey by the U.S. Senate Permanent Subcommittee on Investigations (1984) revealed that about one-third of the states, including the largest and most industrialized, appear to be experiencing the problem. This is all the more significant when one realizes that few states have actually looked for the relationship between organized crime and toxic waste disposal, or even know what to look for. If and when this is done, we may find far more poisoning for profit than we ever imagined.

## CONTROLLING WASTE DISPOSAL

While there is sufficient evidence to generalize about organized crime's national involvement in toxic waste disposal, there is a dearth of solid information on specific cases outside of a few select geographical areas. This situation clearly reflects a history of lax, fumbling, tenuous, and indeed quixotic law enforcement. In fact, more significant prosecutions took place against the purveyors of booze during Prohibition than have taken place against toxic waste dumpers (Nelli, 1976). Though apologists claim that the paltry record reflects the newness of RCRA and toxic waste disposal investigations, most observers agree that the enforcement record is a disgrace (Marino, 1982).

Many dumpers have been encouraged by just the agencies whose mission is first and foremost to protect the public welfare (Marino, 1982). Some state departments of environmental protection and public utility commissions, when faced with the problem of regulating and policing facilities, haulers, and landfills, have chosen to permit harmful, even illegal, practices because they believe no other reasonable choice exists (Marino, 1982). Where is all the garbage going to go, they ask, if they close down a landfill? Who is going to pay to clean up landfills known to be poisoned and the many more suspected? It is such a monstrous headache that their inclination seems to be to avoid as much trouble as possible.

Moreover, behind all these decisions are powerful economic and political forces constantly pressuring regulatory agencies to be, as they put it, reasonable: Work with us, say the lobbyists for the chemical as well as the waste disposal industries, and we can take care of the problems, avoiding onerous regulations and pointless prosecutions which only bring bad publicity. Within this context, we contend that toxic waste dumpers have had an almost open invitation to continue their activities.

Enforcement failures occur for three reasons. First, a regulatory policy of minimal compliance has marked both the Carter and Reagan Administrations' efforts in dealing with toxic waste disposal, encouraged by the belief that states should take the lead in enforcement—a mistaken belief because toxic waste disposal is often an interstate activity. Even the Association of State and Territorial Solid Waste Management Officials has noted that only a strong federal effort, stronger than the first-term Reagan EPA had mustered, could guarantee consistency between state programs and provide the necessary "oversight and auditing" of those programs (Aspen Systems Corporation, 1981: 14–15). Second, political and law enforcement corruption and cronyism have certainly been a feature at the state and local levels, and are suspected at the federal level as well. Finally, a surprising degree of ineptitude has characterized much of the official intelligence-gathering and investigative processes. These three factors feed upon one another. Corruption within state environmental agencies mixes with or is covered up by ineptitude in surveying the problem and vigorously enforcing the laws, and together they thrive under state and federal environmental policies designed to serve the interests of major generators of toxic waste.

State inaction would have been much more difficult to engineer if it did not in many ways match the EPA's stance. It has been federal policy to build a world of environmental regulation dealing with toxic waste disposal, and then to have the regulations enforced by the states. Actually, as government officials admitted privately in interviews with the authors, few believed that the states could or would be able to vigorously enforce environmental laws dealing with toxic waste disposal. This call for devolution to state authorities was primarily a sop to the states' righters in Congress and to those concerned with the growth of the regulatory state; it was also a convenience for federal officials, who could blame non-enforcement on the states.

Toxic waste dumpers are aware that accountability virtually stops at the state line, no matter how much talk there is of federal legislation (U.S. Senate, 1980:III). Hence, they are as pleased with devolution as the most ardent anti-federalist. They know that within states there is, as the New York State Senate Select Committee on Crime put it, more often than not a "benign attitude towards the hazardous waste industry" (New York State Senate, 1981:i). So benign, in fact, that it is much more arduous to get a license to cut hair or drive a cab in most states than to be licensed to haul or store toxic waste. Moreover, sophisticated toxic waste haulers and disposers know how to circumvent the state systems of control and regulation. The New York Select Committee reported on some of the ways this may be done, such as naming fake out-of-state disposal sites on state waste manifests, and transferring toxic waste cargoes from hauler to hauler and site to site using trucks registered to several different corporations located in different states (New York State Senate, 1981:ii). State regulatory and enforcement agencies are ill-equipped to control such practices even when they are inclined to do so.

Congress recognized early that the EPA was footdragging on toxic waste disposal. Several hearings held in the late 1970s established that the EPA was hardly mindful of the need for timely action (U.S. House of Representatives, 1979:1301–1306). During the Carter Administration, the EPA moved at a snail's pace, but it was moving forward. Under the Reagan Administration, at least during the time that Anne Burford was in charge of the EPA, it appeared to move backward.

Perhaps it was only poetic justice that the downfall of Anne Burford and the industry representatives appointed to key staff positions in the EPA came about as the result of toxic waste. When the Reagan Administration assumed office, it began to implement the President's view that there is too much governmental regulation of all aspects of the free enterprise system and that environmental problems are grossly exaggerated. President Reagan once suggested, in fact, that most pollution resulted from vegetation, and that the EPA already had received more money than it could use effectively. He appointed to high offices in the EPA persons who shared his philosophy and were thus disinclined to take aggressive action on ecological problems.

Burford, having virtually no previous experience with environmental issues, and her politically appointed associates, most with backgrounds in industries that had vested interests in EPA regulations, began a program of "regulatory reform." Actually, this meant little more than stripping the agency of its ability to demand compliance with existing legislation. Within a year, the message from EPA was loud and clear: Industry did not have much to worry about from an administration that did not plan to enforce the law (Block and Scarpitti, 1985).

Over the course of the first year and a half of the Burford EPA, enforcement was gutted. This despite the continuing threat posed by organized crime's penetration of the toxic waste industry, which was well known in Washington by that time since Congress had held several highly publicized hearings on organized crime and toxic waste disposal prior to Burford's tenure. What Burford did to the barely emerging program of civil enforcement was to put it through a series of continual reorganizations that left both policies and personnel adrift (U.S. House of Representatives, 1981b:34).

Although the situation was quite bad on the civil enforcement side of the EPA, it was no better in the criminal enforcement program. EPA's lack of criminal investigators was serious enough for the FBI to conclude an agreement with the agency that called for the bureau to investigate 30 toxic waste cases a year. The only problem was that the EPA could not manage to fill the FBI's quota. The agreement was reached in July 1981, and by November 1982, only ten cases had been referred to the FBI. The lack of referrals had no basis in the actual number of cases either known or suspected, but instead reflected a policy of non-compliance with the law that characterized the attitude of top EPA officials (U.S. House of Representatives, 1982).

From one administration to the next, the substantive difference was the ever-increasing boldness by which the agency protected the special interests. It was not that they were unprotected under the Carter Administration, but that the style and degree of protection had now changed. Reagan's EPA was philosophically inclined to find regulation distasteful and crass enough to publicly cater to the polluters.

## LAST THOUGHTS

The hazardous waste disposal industry is inextricably a part of the solid waste or garbage industry, and, as large segments of the solid waste industry are structured by organized crime, so, too, is the hazardous waste industry. As the production of hazardous wastes grew in recent years, and their disposal became increasingly profitable, solid waste entrepreneurs expanded their operations to include substances once handled only by the generators themselves or very specialized carters. When those waste handlers tied to organized crime moved into this new area of operation they brought with them a "business as usual" attitude that allowed practices having possible long-term, detrimental consequences for significant portions of the population to flourish.

As in other areas of organized crime activity, regulations aimed at controlling practices judged to be contrary to the public interest created an illegal market for services. Organized crime filled this demand, both because it typically satisfies illegal demands and because it has extensive involvement in the garbage business. Its entry into and ability to structure the hazardous waste disposal field is neither unexpected nor sudden. It is, however, extremely dangerous. Allowing a significant portion of the social and economic control of a business like hazardous waste disposal to be held by organized crime syndicates is far more devastating for the public well-being than is typically the case for organized crime activity. In fact, the consequences of illegal disposal practices affect many more unknowing and involuntary "victims" than all of organized crime's other illegal operations combined.

The failure of federal and state regulations to keep organized crime out of this industry calls for a serious reexamination of such statutes and the agencies which administer them. And, finally, we would do well to investigate not only the obvious failures catalogued so far, but also how it is that corporate generators of hazardous waste have so artfully escaped both legal responsibility and public opprobrium. The next step in research, therefore, should be the careful scrutiny of the political activities of entities such as the Chemical Manufacturers Association over the past decade or so. What role such powerful lobbyists played in crafting legislation such as RCRA is among the items needing further study. Only then may we be fully able to understand how America's toxic waste racket is the consequence of both illegal disposal practices and the political strength of the petro-chemical industry.

## References

Aspen Systems Corporation (1981). *Hazardous Waste Report*. Rockville, MD (December 14).

Block, Alan A. (1983). "Organized Crime and Toxic Waste—A Summary." In: U.S. Senate, Permanent Subcommittee on Investigations, *Profile of Organized Crime: Mid-Atlantic Region*. Washington, DC: U.S. Government Printing Office.

Block, Alan A. and Frank R. Scarpitti (1985). *Poisoning for Profit: The Mafia and Organized Crime in America*. New York: Morrow.

Brown, Michael (1980). "Drums of Death." *Audubon* (July):120–133.

———— (1981). *Laying Waste: The Poisoning of America by Toxic Chemicals*. New York: Washington Square Press.

Goldstock, Ronald (1985). "Labor Racketeering: A Case Study of the Long Island Carting Industry." Testimony before the President's Commission on Organized Crime, Hearings on Labor Racketeering. Chicago, IL.

Hinchey, Maurice D. (1984). *Criminal Infiltration of the Toxic and Solid Waste Disposal Industries in New York State: Two Case Studies*. New York State Assembly Standing Committee on Environmental Conservation. Albany, NY.

Krajick, Kevin (1981). "When Will Police Discover the Toxic Time Bomb?" *Police Magazine* (May):6–17.

Marino, Ralph J. (1982). *Case History of a Toxic Waste Dumper: The Manipulation of the State Department of Environmental Conservation and the Consequences of Non-Enforcement*. New York State Senate Report. Albany, NY.

McCraw, Thomas K. (1975). "Regulations in America: A Review Article." *Business History Review* 69 (Summer):159–183.

McKenna, J.B. (1983). "Organized Crime in the Toxic Waste Disposal Industry." In: U.S. Senate, Permanent Subcommittee on Investigations, *Profile of Organized Crime: Mid-Atlantic Region*. Washington, DC: U.S. Government Printing Office.

Nelli, Humbert S. (1976). *The Business of Crime: Italians and Syndicate Crime in the United States.* New York: Oxford University Press.

New Jersey Senate. Committee Created Under Senate Resolution No. 4 and Reconstituted Under Senate Resolution No. 3 to Investigate the Cost of Garbage Collection and Disposal (1959). *Hearings.* Trenton, NJ.

New Jersey Special Legislative Commission (1969). *Public Hearing to Investigate Certain Problems Relating to Solid Waste Disposal.* Trenton, NJ.

New Jersey Superior Court (1980a). *State of New Jersey v. Duane Marine Salvage Corporation*, Indictment No. 71-80-4.

———— (1980b). *State of New Jersey v. New Jersey Trade*, Indictment, State Grand Jury No. SGJ-66-80-8.

New York State Senate Select Committee on Crime (1980). "In the Matter of Public Hearing on Organized Crime and Toxic Waste." Testimony of John Fine (July 8).

———— (1981). *An Investigation into Illegal Hazardous Waste Disposal on Long Island: An Interim Report* (February 25).

New York State Supreme Court (1984). *County of Suffolk, People of the State of New York v. Corallo*, Indictment No. 1472-84.

Reich, Charles A. (1964). "The New Property." *Yale Law Review* 73 (April):733–787.

*Resource Conservation and Recovery Act* (RCRA) (1976), 42 U.S.C. 6901–6987.

Reuter, Peter (n.d.). *Conspiracy Among the Many: A Study of Racketeers as Cartel Organizers.* Washington, DC: Rand. Mimeographed.

Savas, E.S. (1977). *The Organization and Efficiency of Solid Waste Collection.* Lexington, MA: D.C. Heath.

Shabecoff, Philip (1983). "Chemical Leaders Hear Public Fear is Top Problem." *New York Times* (June 10).

U.S. District Court. District of New Jersey (1981). *United States v. Price & Proctor & Gamble Co.*, Civil Action No. 80-4104 (September 22).

U.S. House of Representatives (1979). *Hazardous Waste Disposal.* Hearings Before the Subcommittee on Oversight and Investigations of the Committee on Interstate and Foreign Commerce. Washington, DC: U.S. Government Printing Office.

———— (1980). *Organized Crime and Hazardous Waste Disposal.* Hearing Before the Subcommittee on Oversight and Investigations of the Committee on Interstate and Foreign Commerce. Washington, DC: U.S. Government Printing Office.

————, Subcommittee on Oversight and Investigations of the Committee on Energy and Commerce. (1981a). *Hazardous Waste Matters: A*

*Case Study of Landfill Sites.* Washington, DC: U.S. Government
Printing Office.

_____ (1981b). *Organized Crime Links to the Waste Disposal Industry.*
Hearing Before the Subcommittee on Oversight and Investiga-
tions of the Committee on Energy and Commerce. Washington,
DC: U.S. Government Printing Office.

_____ (1982). *Hazardous Waste Enforcement.* Report of the Subcommittee on Oversight and Investigations of the Committee on
Energy and Commerce. Washington, DC: U.S. Government Printing Office.

U.S. Senate, Permanent Subcommittee on Investigations (1984). "Staff
Summary, State Attorneys' General Hazardous Waste Survey."

U.S. Senate, Select Committee on Improper Activities in the Labor or
Management Field (1957). *Investigation of Improper Activities
in the Labor or Management Field.* Washington, DC: U.S. Government Printing Office.

U.S. Senate, Subcommittee on Oversight of Government Management of
the Committee on Governmental Affairs (1980). *Report on
Hazardous Waste Management and the Implementation of the
Resource Conservation and Recovery Act.* Washington, DC: U.S.
Government Printing Office.

Wilheim, Georgina K. (1981). "The Regulation of Hazardous Waste
Disposal: Cleaning Up the Augean Stables with a Flood of Regulations." *Rutgers Law Review* 33:906–972.

# Unusual Crime or Crime as Usual? Images of Corruption at the Interstate Commerce Commission*

## Merry Morash
## and Donna Hale

*Media coverage of the corruption of U.S. Interstate Commerce Commission (ICC) officials presents a selective picture of their crimes. The news emphasized individual acts of corruption and organized crime involvement at the cost of obscuring an understanding of organizational deviance. Although news coverage is not intended to serve as social science data, academics as well as the general public often use media portrayals to support their own theories on crime. Such a reliance can and does undermine progress in criminological theory, especially in the area of organized crime.*

In the late 1970s, a considerable amount of news coverage centered on alleged corruption of governmental employees at the U.S. Interstate Commerce Commission (ICC), which is the federal agency charged with

*Authors' Note: An earlier version of this paper was presented at the September 1982 Meetings of the Society for the Study of Social Problems, San Francisco. The authors would like to thank Edward Morash, Professor of Marketing and Transportation at Michigan State University, for his extensive consultation in carrying out the research; Malcolm Spector at the Department of Sociology, University of Montreal, for comments on the earlier version of the paper; and Cheryl Saylor at Michigan State University for her assistance in data collection. Freedom of Information Act specialist, Kathy Semone, at the Federal Merit System Protection Board, and James K. Hall, the Chief of the FBI Records Management Division, also were of considerable help in obtaining documents.

the economic regulation of surface transportation (truck, rail, and barge). The ICC's major regulatory activities have included approving rates, mergers and acquisitions, and granting operating authorities that permit hauling of specified commodities in specific geographic areas. The news coverage focused on Robert L. Oswald, who was director of the ICC Office of the Secretary for Congressional Relations, and his deputy, Richard W. Kyle. These two men were accused of giving special favors to several companies regulated by the ICC, and allegations were made that organized crime was involved in the corruption.

Prior research has shown that crime news generally presents a selective perception of reality. On the one hand, newspapers have been found to overemphasize serious crimes, particularly those involving violence, sex and indecency (Roshier, 1973; Ditton and Duffy, 1983; Sherizen, 1978). On the other hand, there is evidence that newspapers deemphasize corporate and other business crimes, in part because their focus is on the illegal activities of individuals, particularly street criminals, rather than on organizations (Evans and Lundman, 1983; Sutherland, 1949; Coleman, 1974; Molotch and Lester, 1975; Graber, 1980; Fishman, 1978; Quinney, 1979). Generalizing these findings to the Oswald and Kyle cases, we would expect news accounts to stress the individual deviance of both men and the people who corrupted them, but to deemphasize the role that organizational or economic structures might play in perpetuating a widespread pattern of corruption.

News accounts have been found to introduce distortions in ways other than their emphasis on individual crime. The news usually does not explicitly identify the causes and the related remedies for criminal activity (Dussuyer, 1978; Graber, 1980; Sherizen, 1978; and summary by Garofalo, 1981), but through the juxtaposition of simultaneously occurring events it often implies crime patterns, causes, and remedies. In this vein, there is a tendency to introduce distortion by presenting discrete events as part of an orderly pattern, or by linking them to the same general theme (Cohen, 1973; McCann, 1973; Fishman, 1978). For example, Fishman (1978:535) described a newspaper editor who organized stories about several crime incidents and law enforcement responses under the general heading of violence against the elderly. Subsequently, with the cooperation of the police, news reporters sought out more stories about violence against the elderly, and a crime wave was "created" in the news independent of any change in the actual frequency of crimes against the elderly. Finally, newspapers tend to neglect developments that unfold gradually, at least until they reach some dramatic point such as the arrest of a suspect or punishment of a criminal (Rock, 1973; Murdock, 1973). Using the terms in the title of this article, the newspaper emphasis is on unusual crime, not crime as usual. If a person has a lengthy criminal career, or an organization has a continuing history of corruption, these patterns are typically ignored until a dramatic moment when some part of the chain of events constitutes a newsworthy story.

Although the news coverage of crime is of interest in itself, coverage of organized crime is of particular interest because it shapes not only public but also some academic understanding. News accounts of organized crime activity have a significant influence in academia because, probably more than in any other area of criminological research, they have been accepted as data sources. Galliher and Cain (1974) showed that textbooks commonly cite news stories as evidence of the activities of organized crime figures. Moreover, Bequai's (1979:165) book on organized crime cited newspaper coverage of the ICC story and of scandals at other regulatory agencies as the major source of information from which he concluded that "corrupt practices by bureaucrats are so common in many cities that criminal syndicates do not need to offer temptations." In this way, the picture of organized crime and corruption that is established in the news influences the views of college and university students, who often become criminal justice practitioners and policy-makers.

The purpose of studying media coverage of the corruption at the ICC is to demonstrate how the selection and presentation of information develops a particular image of illegal activity and its causes. The nature of this picture is quite predictable from the prior research reviewed above on the news coverage of crime.

## METHODOLOGY

Our examination of the news coverage of the Oswald and Kyle story centered on three big city newspapers, the *New York Times*, the *Washington Post*, and the *Chicago Tribune*; the major business-oriented newspaper in the nation, the *Wall Street Journal*; and the main independent weekly magazine covering the transportation industry, *Traffic World*.

A content analysis was carried out on all of the articles published in the five news media between 1977 and 1979 pertaining to corruption at the ICC. The presence and amount of material in each article were coded for the following topics: Oswald's alleged offense; Kyle's alleged offense; investigations by the U.S. Department of Justice (DOJ), Federal Bureau of Investigation (FBI), and grand jury; the ICC internal investigation; ICC findings and/or decision to fire Oswald and/or Kyle; Oswald's and/or

Kyle's appeal to the U.S. Federal Merit System Protection Board; results of the Federal Merit System Protection Board appeal; indictment of Oswald; Oswald's trial before the federal district court; results of the federal district court trial; and appeal to the U.S. Circuit Court of Appeals for the District of Columbia. Additional topics were: organized crime; use of the terms "Mafia" or "La Cosa Nostra"; and descriptions of other criminal activity beside the alleged corrupt acts of Oswald and Kyle. The emphasis on each topic in the headlines also was examined.

Two other data sources helped establish the degree to which the news reports omitted or selectively emphasized some of the available information on corruption at the ICC. The first was the U.S. Federal Merit System Protection Board (FMSPB) hearing transcripts, available through the Freedom of Information Act, of Oswald's appeal of the ICC decision to fire him. Such records of court proceedings are often an important source of reporters' information on illegal activities (Rock, 1973; Fishman, 1978); several of the stories examined were centered on coverage of the hearings, which were open to the public.

The second source of information was the transcript of the 1978 U.S. Senate Hearings Before the Subcommittee on Antitrust Monopoly of the Committee on the Judiciary. Some of the testimony at these hearings focused on the ICC, and the hearings took place at the same time that the Oswald and Kyle cases were being investigated. During the hearings, Senator Edward Kennedy and the commissioner of the ICC both alluded to Oswald and Kyle, but they did not discuss the scandal specifically because the investigation was under way. However, numerous other acts of possible wrongdoing at the ICC were the subject of testimony.


## FINDINGS

Our search for news stories revealed that *Traffic World* devoted the greatest number of articles, 20, to wrongdoing at the ICC. The *Washington Post* published 15 articles, and the *New York Times* 12. There were three articles in the *Wall Street Journal* and two in the *Chicago Tribune*.

### Individual Criminal Activity

On the whole, and consistent with prior research, our data revealed a predominant emphasis on specific improper acts by Oswald and Kyle. Oswald's alleged offenses were the most frequently mentioned of any of the topics studied, with 41 (79%) of the 52 articles containing some information on his activities (Table 1). A smaller proportion (24 or 46%) of the articles recounted Kyle's alleged offenses; the *Wall Street Journal* and the *Chicago Tribune* did not cover the story about Kyle at all. The

**Table 1**
Number and Proportion of Articles
Including Information on Each Topic

|  | *Traffic World* | *Wall Street Journal* | *New York Times* | *Washington Post* | *Chicago Tribune* | *Total* |
|---|---|---|---|---|---|---|
| Oswald's alleged offenses | 15 (75%) | 2 (33.3%) | 7 (56%) | 14 (93.3%) | 2 (100%) | 40 (79%) |
| Kyle's alleged offenses | 12 (60%) | 0 (0%) | 6 (50%) | 6 (40%) | 0 (0%) | 24 (46%) |
| DOJ, FBI, grand jury investigations | 15 (75%) | 1 (50%) | 6 (50%) | 8 (67%) | 1 (33%) | 31 (60%) |
| ICC Investigations | 15 (75%) | 0 (0%) | 0 (0%) | 8 (67) | 0 (0%) | 23 (44%) |
| ICC accusations and firing | 17 (85%) | 0 (0%) | 6 (50%) | 13 (87%) | 1 (50%) | 37 (71%) |
| Request for ICC hearing | 1 (5%) | 0 (0%) | 0 (0%) | 1 (7%) | 0 (0%) | 2 (4%) |
| Appeal to Merit System Protection Board | 13 (65%) | 0 (0%) | 4 (33%) | 7 (47%) | 0 (0%) | 24 (46%) |
| Results of Merit System Protection Board appeal | 1 (5%) | 0 (0%) | 0 (0%) | 1 (7%) | 0 (0%) | 2 (4%) |
| Oswald's indictment | 4 (20%) | 1 (33%) | 1 (8%) | 6 (50%) | 1 (50%) | 13 (25%) |
| Federal District Court trial | 4 (20%) | 0 (0%) | 0 (0%) | 2 (13%) | 0 (0%) | 6 (11.5%) |
| Results of Federal District Court trial | 2 (10%) | 1 (33%) | 1 (8%) | 2 (13%) | 0 (0%) | 6 (11.5%) |
| Appeal to the US Court of Appeals for the District of Columbia and result | 1 (5%) | 0 (0%) | 0 (0%) | 0 (0%) | 0 (0%) | 1 (1.9%) |
| Link to organized crime | 11 (55%) | 1 (33.3%) | 8 (66.7%) | 15 (100%) | 2 (100%) | 37 (71%) |
| Mafia | 0 (0%) | 0 (0%) | 1 (8.3%) | 7 (46.7%) | 0 (0%) | 8 (15%) |
| Other crimes | 2 (10%) | 0 (0%) | 3 (25%) | 3 (20%) | 0 (0%) | 8 (15.4) |
| Total number of articles | 20 | 3 | 12 | 15 | 2 | 52 |

amount of coverage devoted to Oswald's and Kyle's offenses was relatively large, averaging 109 words and 56 words respectively. These word counts represent a high proportion of the average article, which was 444 words long.

The particular illegal act mentioned varied over time since the different investigations and hearings centered on somewhat different allegations. Initially, the FBI, DOJ, and grand jury investigations concentrated on allegations that Oswald and Kyle had facilitated a reversal in a decision to grant a permanent operating authority, had given some trucking companies advance notice of ICC decisions, and had given preferential treatment to some companies by assisting their officers in obtaining favorable rulings from the ICC. Subsequent to the investigations, a grand jury indicted Oswald for accepting $4,000 in cash, two trips to resorts, and three cases of liquor in exchange for helping the Consolidated Carrier Corporation, a trucking firm, to obtain an operating authority. Apart from the FBI, DOJ, and grand jury investigations, the ICC used its own evidence as the basis for charging Oswald with violating the Hatch Act by taking an active part in a congressional political campaign, obstructing justice by failing to cooperate with the DOJ investigation, providing members of Congress with advance notice of ICC decisions, and giving preferential treatment to private attorneys who handled ICC cases. Kyle was accused of accepting gifts, food, drink, lodging, and travel from officials of a trucking company. Although the specifics of Oswald's and Kyle's illegal activities depend on the investigation being covered, in all cases we are left with the impression of two government officials acting in a highly irregular and illegal fashion.

The focus on Oswald and Kyle as individual wrongdoers also was reflected in the references to them in the headlines (Table 2). All of the headlines in *Traffic World*, the *Wall Street Journal*, and the *Chicago Tribune* mentioned Oswald and/or Kyle by name and/or specification of their position. Nine (75%) of the 12 *New York Times* headlines referred to Oswald and/or Kyle, and 12 (80%) of the 15 *Washington Post* headlines referred to them.

Consistent with prior research findings that reporters rely heavily on official statements by representatives of criminal justice agencies (Rock, 1973; Fishman, 1978), the news reports mirror the ICC attorneys and the Federal Merit System Protection Board hearing examiner's position that Oswald and Kyle committed isolated illegal acts. The official position is apparent in one ICC attorney's statement about the appropriateness of calling witnesses to testify concerning widespread, possibly illegal practices at the ICC: "It's not the Interstate Commerce Commission that's on trial here." The hearing examiner similarly restricted

**Table 2**

Headlines for Stories on the Oswald and Kyle Cases

| Major Topic | Traffic World | Wall Street Journal | New York Times | Washington Post | Chicago Tribune |
|---|---|---|---|---|---|
| Initial Investigations | 6/13/77: "Two Top ICC Officials Part of Investigation by D of J, FBI, Grand Jury" | 6/6/77: "ICC Aides Investigated By Federal Grand Jury" | 6/4/77: "Two ICC Officials Under Investigation" <br><br> 6/5/77: "Justice Aides Link New York City Trucker to Inquiry on ICC" <br><br> 6/9/77: "ICC Puts 2 Aides On Leave in Inquiry Related to Trucking" <br><br> 5/18/77: "Rep. Murphy Says He Gave Aid in '72 to Son of Gambino" <br><br> 7/6/77: "Organized Crime on Capital Hill Is Focus of a Wide Inquiry Spawned by ICC Case" | 6/4/77: "Grand Jury Is Probing ICC Moves: US Investigation Centers on Advance Word of Decisions" | |

135

## Table 2 (Continued)
### Headlines for Stories on the Oswald and Kyle Cases

| Major Topic | Traffic World | Wall Street Journal | New York Times | Washington Post | Chicago Tribune |
|---|---|---|---|---|---|
| | 9/5/77: "Oswald, Kyle to Return to ICC Under New Duties for Not Over 4 Months" | | | | |
| Reactions by Oswald, Kyle, and the ICC to initial investigations | 12/5/77: "Figure in ICC Probe Seeks Early Retirement Based on 'Disability' " | | | | |
| | 12/19/77: "Oswald Told ICC Intends to Fire Him, Given Until Dec. 23 to Make Reply" | | | | |
| | 1/9/78: "Oswald Answers Notice of Termination, Makes ICC's Charges Public" | | 1/5/78: "Accused ICC Official Seeks Public Hearing Charges Include Effort to Influence Organized Crime Case Witness" | 1/4/78: "Charges Against Oswald by ICC Detailed, Denied" | 1/5/78: "ICC Aide Accused of Probe Tampering" |
| Oswald Is Fired | 1/16/78: "Oswald Fired from ICC; He Will File Appeal, Seek Hearings at Civil Service" | | 1/10/78: "Controversial Official on ICC Staff Dismissed" | 1/10/78: "ICC Rejects Ex-Staff's Appeal" | |

136

# Table 2 (Continued)
## Headings for Stories on the Oswald and Kyle Cases

| Major Topic | Traffic World | Wall Street Journal | New York Times | Washington Post | Chicago Tribune |
|---|---|---|---|---|---|
| | 6/12/78: "Oswald Getting Federal Disability Pay; Kyle Withdraws Resignation" | | 6/8/78: "Ex-Aide Withdraws Resignation in Further Dispute with ICC" | 6/8/78: "Resignation Withdrawn, Kyle is Fired by ICC" | |
| | 6/12/78: "ICC Tells Kyle He's Fired Within Hours After He Withdraws Resignation" | | 7/14/78: "ICC Official Ousted on Misconduct Charges" | 6/7/78: "Kyle Resigns His ICC Post Amid Charge He Took Gifts" | |
| | | | 7/15/78: "ICC Aide Dismissed." | | |
| Kyle Is Fired | 7/24/78: "Kyle Dismissal by ICC Made Effective July 14; Appeal to CSC Planned" | | | 7/14/78: "ICC Head, Members of Staff Accused" | |
| | | | | 8/27/73: "Influence and Murder: Probe of ICC Raises New Questions" | |
| | 10/2/78: "Former Secretary of ICC Indicted; Hearing Before CSC on Firing Begun" | 9/25/78: "Former ICC Official Is Indicted on Charges of Accepting Bribes" | 9/24/78: "Indictment"  12/22/78: "Ex-ICC Officer is Cleared of Influence Peddling" | 9/23/78: "US Jury Indicts Central Figure in Probe of ICC" | 9/23/78: "ICC Ex-Official Indicted in Bribery, Fraud Probe" |

**Table 2 (Continued)**

Headlines for Stories on the Oswald and Kyle Cases

| Major Topic | Traffic World | Wall Street Journal | New York Times | Washington Post | Chicago Tribune |
|---|---|---|---|---|---|
| | 10/9/78: "Oswald Pleads Not Guilty to US Criminal Charges; Kyle Appeal Hearing Set" | 12/26/78: "Former ICC Official Acquitted of Charges He Accepted Bribes" | | 9/26/78: "Oswald Abused Position at at ICC, Hearing Is Told" | |
| | 10/16/78: "Gresham of ICC Refuses to Testify at Oswald's Appeal of His Firing" | | | 9/28/78: "Attorney Hits Case Against Official at ICC" | |
| | 10/23/78: "FEAA Upholds Ruling that Gresham of ICC Must Testify at Oswald's Hearing" | | | 9/30/78: "Oswald Claims Innocence at Arraignment" | |
| Appeals and Trials | 10/30/78: "Oswald's Hearing Ends Amid Charges of 'Paranoia' and 'Chicanery'" | | | 10/24/78: "Sex, Booze and Organized Crime; Appeals Board Hears ICC Testimony" | |
| | 11/6/78: "O'Neal Says Allegations by Kyle Had No Influence on ICC's Firing Decisions" | | | 12/14/78: "Oswald Private Lobbyist Jury told" | |
| | | | | 12/22/78: "ICC Ex-Official Acquitted: Influence-Peddling Bribery Trial" | |

## Table 2 (Continued)
### Headlines for Stories on the Oswald and Kyle Cases

| Major Topic | Traffic World | Wall Street Journal | New York Times | Washington Post | Chicago Tribune |
|---|---|---|---|---|---|
| | 11/6/78: "Kyle's Attorneys Argue Limits on Evidence Hamper Defense" | | | | |
| | 1/15/79: "Oswald of ICC Acquitted on Criminal Charges of Bribery Conspiracy" | | | | |
| Oswald's and Kyle's Final Attempts to Return to the ICC | 1/15/79: "Oswald Seeks Restoration to His Former Position as Commissioner's Secretary" | | | 3/6/79: "Board Upholds ICC Dismissal of Secretary" | |
| | 3/12/79: "Board Upholds ICC Firing of Oswald, Kyle, Drops Certain ICC Allegations" | | | | |
| | 11/19/79: "Appeals Court Dismisses Oswald, Kyle Pleas to Overturn ICC Removals" | | | | |

139

the testimony of previous employees about long-standing, questionable practices: "If they weren't employed at the time the gentleman [Oswald] was in the role, their testimony would be meaningless." Because the hearing procedure had the manifest objective of determining whether Oswald and Kyle as individuals were rightfully terminated from employment, it is not surprising that the news accounts, which had the hearings as a primary source of information, emphasized individual rather than bureaucracy-wide wrongdoing. News stories gave little attention to Oswald's position that he did not deviate from organizational norms.

## The Organized Crime Connection

Although no news medium regularly portrayed the activities of Oswald or Kyle as part of any pattern of illegal activity in government bureaucracy, two extensive feature articles did draw a picture of complex interconnections between gangsters, many different kinds of corruption, and illegal acts of bureaucrats and various unsavory characters. The most extensive *New York Times* articles (6/7/77) described the interconnections between several different people engaged in illegal activity (Table 3). In this network, Thomas Gambino, owner of Consolidated Carriers Corporation, is indirectly connected with Oswald and Kyle, and with the Washington lobbyist Merle D. Baumgart, through Gambino's lawyer Martin R. Martino, who frequently socialized with the three men. Oswald also is directly connected to Gambino by their alleged meeting to discuss Gambino's application for an operating authority, and he is tied to Baumgart through an exchange of financial assistance and during a period when they shared an apartment.

In an examination of events surrounding Baumgart's death, the feature article revealed a network of interconnections so complicated that it is difficult to picture. Baumgart was killed in a suspicious traffic accident after telling friends that his life was threatened. A person named Daryl E. Fleming called Martino to inform him of Baumgart's death, and Martino then called the maitre d'hotel at the Rotunda Restaurant, where Baumgart had eaten just before his death, to request that Baumgart's check be held. The maitre d'hotel, Alixis A. Goodarzi, was later killed in what the feature article reported as a "gangland" type of shooting. Further, Fleming previously had conspired in a bribery that involved federal accreditation of vocational schools. One of his co-conspirators was a congressional aide (Steven Elko), who had sponsored the naturalization of Goodarzi and allegedly arranged numerous meetings between congressmen and prostitutes that were paid for by organized crime figures. In keeping with tendencies for news sources to echo each other

**Table 3**

A Network of People and Actions Described by the *New York Times*

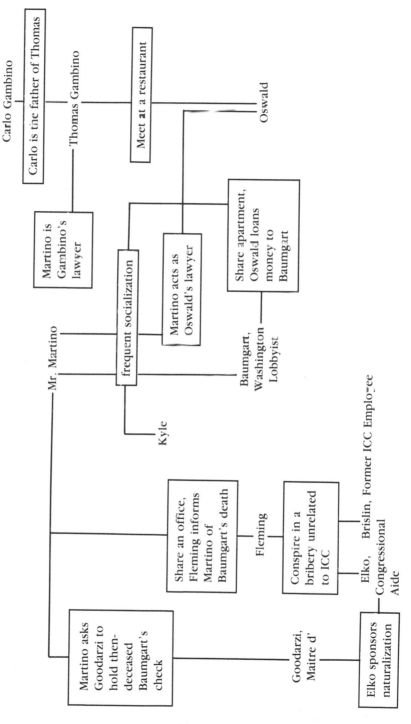

(Rock, 1973:77–78; Fishman, 1978:534, 537), and reinforcing the image of an organized crime network, part of the elaborate *New York Times* picture was described in a *Washington Post* feature article (8/27/78). Also, one *Traffic World* article (6/13/77) on Oswald mentioned the DOJ investigation of the deaths of Goodarzi and Baumgart, but did not explain how they were connected to Oswald or to any other aspect of the investigation. The net effect of describing the complicated interconnections is to insinuate that corruption at the ICC is linked to organized crime's prostitution enterprise, as well as government-wide corruption of civil servants by organized crime and gangland killings.

Beside the *New York Times* and *Washington Post* feature stories, and the sections that were reproduced in *Traffic World*, shorter references to organized crime involvement in the corruption at the ICC figure prominently in the news accounts studied. In fact, the reported connection between the ICC corruption and organized crime was second in quantity of coverage only to recapitulations of Oswald's alleged offenses. Among the 52 articles, 37 (71%) noted or explained a connection between ICC corruption and organized crime, and 8 (15%) specifically used the term "Mafia"; none used the term "La Cosa Nostra." In many instances, the reference to organized crime was short, often consisting of just a phrase to indicate that Thomas Gambino, owner of Consolidated Carriers Corporation, was "the son of the underworld leader, Carlo Gambino," or that Dowd, who headed the DOJ investigation, was "an expert in organized crime cases." Longer references to organized crime were included in two *New York Times* articles, the first (6/5/77) stating that the "St. Paul–Minneapolis area has reportedly been the center of alleged corrupt trucking practices and of links between trucking unions and crime syndicates"; and the second article (6/5/77) noting that "The New York City garment district trucking industry was one of the targets of an earlier 18-month investigation called Project Cleveland, by the Federal Joint Strike Force Against Organized Crime." In addition to these references, three *New York Times* headlines (6/18/77; 7/6/77; 1/5/78) and one *Washington Post* headline (10/24/78) specifically referred to organized crime or an organized crime figure. Overall, the *Washington Post*, the *New York Times* and, to some extent, *Traffic World* highlighted the connection of organized crime with the Oswald and Kyle cases more than did either the *Chicago Tribune* or the *Wall Street Journal*. Yet, all of the news sources established some relationship.

Another way in which the news conveyed the impression of a proven link between organized crime and the corruption of Oswald and Kyle was through its emphasis on allegations rather than hearing outcomes. All of the news media covered the initial FBI, DOJ, and grand jury investigations and Oswald's indictment (Table 1). However, only *Traffic World* and the *Washington Post* reported that the Federal Merit System Protection Board found that the ICC decision to fire Oswald and Kyle was justified on the following limited set of charges: Oswald had given preferential treatment to Consolidated Carriers by meeting with the company's owner and lawyer; Oswald had obstructed justice by asking the attorney not to tell DOJ investigators about the meeting; and Kyle had accepted food, drink, lodging, travel, and gifts from a regulated carrier.

The major source of information about organized crime that was available to the public, and thus to reporters, was the testimony before the Federal Merit System Protection Board. Unlike the news reports, the testimony falls far short of establishing the responsibility of organized crime for the corruption of Oswald and Kyle. The most direct reference to the Mafia was testimony about Oswald's and Congressman John M. Murphy's attempts to assure Theodore Polydoroff, who eventually became Gambino's lawyer, that the Gambino brothers had no Mafia involvement.

Another way that the topic of organized crime came up at the Federal Merit System Protection Board hearing was in references to the FBI and grand jury investigations of Oswald. Yet, the impression of Oswald's and Kyle's involvement with organized crime is not substantiated in the Federal Merit System Protection Board testimony. The testimony at the U.S. Senate hearings (1978), the other main source of information on corruption at the ICC, similarly does not reveal an organized crime connection.

**Patterns of Wrongdoing at the ICC**

Only four of the news articles examine alleged patterns of ICC corruption not involving organized crime. These articles are based on accusations by Oswald and/or Kyle that, like themselves, the ICC chairman and other government officials had repeatedly violated the ICC Canons of Conduct governing gift-taking and providing assistance to carriers. In contrast to the scant newspaper coverage, the testimony before the Federal Merit System Protection Board repeatedly reveals that several of the activities for which Oswald and Kyle were admonished were so common that many employees considered them to be "business as usual" at the ICC. In this vein, ICC Administrative Law Judge Mittlebronn said that in his opinion it would be legal for Oswald to provide a firm with the names of six or a dozen lawyers. Several other people familiar with ICC operations over many years gave testimony that it was a "very common practice" for the secretary and field members of the ICC to furnish names of attorneys, that it was "long standing practice," and that it was common practice whenever there was a persistent request.

Consistent with responses to questions about the list of attorneys, the responses to questions about assistance to attorneys repeatedly revealed that this practice was routine, and indeed a recognized function of the ICC staff. In particular, Administrative officer Edward C. Fernandez testified that it is "common practice in the office" to give attorneys advice, and that several attorneys "appear frequently" at the ICC office. A member of the clerical staff also stated that the official function of Oswald's assistant secretary was to aid attorneys representing cases before the ICC, and the assistant secretary described his fequent help to attorneys in locating relevant cases with the law indexes at the ICC office.

Additionally, there was no disagreement during the Federal Merit System Protection Board hearing that the ICC Congressional Liaison Office regularly provided advance notice of its decisions to members of Congress. Employees at every level described the practice as "very common." Two secretaries in Oswald's office independently stated that they took requests for advance releases to members of Congress "all the time," and that the recognized purpose was to allow the senators and representatives to do "simultaneous releases" with the ICC office.

In further support of the view that the receipt of favors and gifts from regulated carriers was widespread at the ICC, Senator Edward Kennedy summarized testimony before a congressional subcommittee as follows: ". . . as the [Interstate Commerce] Commission's own investigations, as well as the subcommittee's investigations, have shown, the recipients of carrier gifts and payments include not only shippers but also personnel of government agencies, including the ICC itself . . . The evidence of gifts and entertainment given to certain ICC personnel raises even more troubling doubts about the Commission's ability to scrutinize motor carrier rates free from undue influence" (U.S. Senate, 1978:903). Kennedy's summary was based on evidence presented by five current and former ICC auditors from governmental regional offices. A partial list of the auditors' findings includes evidence that:

1. One carrier listed 22 luncheons with ICC staff during a two-year period.

2. One carrier listed gifts valued at under $10 to eight ICC employees.

3. One ICC employee who was charged with *ex parte* communications involving coercion for grants of applications was simply reprimanded in a letter.

4. One carrier employee arrived at the ICC office during the Christmas season and helped an ICC employee take a gift of a case of liquor to his car.

5. A Pittsburgh ICC employee received the equivalent of $1,200 from one carrier in the form of a $25 gift certificate, golf outings, and other weekend entertainment.

Because there are fewer than 60 auditors to check on at least 6,000 carriers, it is likely that the extent of the problem was even more widespread than the auditors reported. In contrast to news emphasis on the role of organized crime figures, the auditors did not indicate that a large proportion, or indeed any of the illegal activities by carriers involved organized crime.

## Causes of Corruption

None of the 52 news articles provided any explicit analysis of the causes of Oswald's or Kyle's activities, or of corruption in the trucking industry or the ICC. However, the predominant emphases suggested that corruption is caused by personal failings and by organized crime figures who are external to both the ICC and the usual operations of the economy.

In contrast to causal implications drawn from the news, the U.S. Senate hearings (1978:903) focused on structural conditions that can explain widespread corruption. Because trucking is regulated, carriers usually belong to rate bureaus that establish the rates to be approved by the ICC. One result of this practice is that carriers tend not to compete by changing their rates. Instead, they resort to either excess services that shippers might prefer to forego in exchange for lower rates, or to the illegal practice of giving gifts and entertainment to shippers. Another form of competition is the provision of gifts and entertainment to ICC employees in exchange for information and favorable ICC decisions.

In an earlier period, a Ralph Nader group report put forth another structural explanation of illegal activity at the ICC. Rather than serving its intended function—"to protect and represent the public interest in matters of transportation in interstate commerce"—the report concludes that the ICC actually serves as "a forum at which transportation interests divide up the national transportation market" (Fellmeth, 1970). Due in part to the high cost of litigation, smaller carriers and individual consumers are excluded from using this forum, but larger firms are involved in persistent "personal lobbying" to influence transportation policy and specific ICC decisions. Like the 1978 U.S. Senate hearings, the Nader report portrayed the entire ICC organization as tending to take part in illegal activity and as holding a deviant role in a network of interrelationships with members of Congress and transportation firms.

## CONCLUSIONS AND DISCUSSION

According to news accounts of wrongdoing at the ICC, Oswald and Kyle were corrupted by organized crime figures who had infiltrated legitimate firms. The view that organized crime and corruption are alien to usual economic activity is consistent with the general assumption that crime is an unusual disruption in an otherwise smoothly functioning social and economic structure (e.g., Hall, *et al.*, 1978:55). This view of crime as an unusual event, resulting from the failings of particular ICC staff and business operators, reflected the official position of the ICC and the hearing examiner for the Federal Merit System Protection Board.

A broader picture of the illegal activities at the ICC is offered by the defense testimony before the Federal Merit System Protection Board and by the testimony in the U.S. Senate (1978). These sources suggest that Oswald's and Kyle's activities were part of a widespread and generally accepted pattern of exchange among ICC staff, members of Congress, transportation firms and their attorneys. In particular, long-standing interactions between members of Congress, ICC staff, and the carriers who are the Congress's constituents, provide the context in which ICC staff members assist firms that they are regulating. The Federal Merit System Protection Board testimony reveals a pattern in which trucking firm owners ask their senators and representatives to help them in their dealings with the ICC. In response, members of Congress request aid from the ICC Congressional Liaison Officer. Thus, Congressional control over the ICC budget and powers makes it possible for senators and representatives to seek information and assistance for firms in their districts from the very agency that is established to regulate these firms.

Another factor influencing ICC staff to take on roles other than unyielding advocacy for the public good is the network of personal ties between ICC staff, attorneys who represent cases before the ICC, and members of Congress. The rather frequent exchanges of employees between the ICC, law firms that represent clients before the ICC, and trucking firms regulated by the ICC, form the basis of these ties. For example, Gambino's lawyer was employed by the ICC and shared an office with Oswald before he was employed by a law firm to represent clients before the ICC.

It is clear that the image of a few individuals corrupted by organized crime figures does not give a full picture of wrongdoing at the ICC. The broader pattern of illegal activity is most accurately described as organizational deviance (Ermann and Lundman, 1978:7–8; Reiss, 1983:79), a categorization based on two factors: ICC employees' acceptance of gifts and favors qualifies as "contrary to norms maintained by others outside the organization"; and these actions appear to be "supported by the internal operating norms of the organization," as evidenced by the widely recognized but usually unpunished exchange of favors and gifts (Ermann and Lundman, 1978).

The news images can best be understood and anticipated by recognizing two ways in which available information is selectively assembled into news reports. First, news accounts do not take an adequate sampling of either illegal acts or actors; they emphasize discrete events and individuals' crimes rather than organizational crime. This tendency results, in part, from the reflection in the news of the official position of the government—in this case the ICC and the Federal Merit System Protection Board.

Second, the news often stresses temporal and spatial interrelationships between people and actions, as exemplified by Figure 3, rather than interactions between people that can explain how an illegal activity came to pass. Specifically, the news accounts, particularly the feature news stories, depicted the corruption of Oswald and Kyle as illegal actions embedded in a network of interrelationships between organized crime figures, other lawbreaking government employees, and illegal acts thought to be typical of organized crime, such as bribery and gangland killings. But none of the news accounts revealed key interactions between the associated individuals. For example, there is no evidence of conversations between Oswald or Kyle and members of an organized crime group.

In contrast, the U.S. Senate hearings (1978) and the Federal Merit System Protection Board testimony did place the illegal activities at the ICC in the context of two networks of relationships that were not mentioned in the news: a network including ICC staff, members of Congress, and firm representatives; and a network consisting of ICC staff, lawyers representing firms before the ICC, and representatives of regulated firms. Unlike the news, the testimony provided considerable information about conversations and other exchanges that occurred among the people in these networks. Thus, the networks help explain how, for example, an exchange of favors, gifts, or information could be coordinated and justified.

In sum, the news provided only a partial understanding of corruption at the ICC. It emphasized unusual individual acts of criminality and the linkage to organized crime, but ignored the degree to which corruption is part of a pattern of "business as usual." Alternative sources suggest that the ICC can be characterized as a deviant organization, and that structural factors, specifically the relations between the ICC, Congress, trucking firms and their legal representatives might explain the widespread collusion between ICC staff and regulated firms.

To the degree that the news helps to shape public and academic understanding of the causes of corruption, it can influence the choice of a control policy stressing either the identification of organized crime figures and corrupt government workers, or structural conditions that are conducive to widespread illegal activity. Thus, it is of considerable importance to identify and explain the imagery that is created in the news.

## References

Bequai, August (1979). *Organized Crime*. Lexington, MA: Lexington Books.

Cohen, Stanley (1973). "Mods and Rockers: The Inventory as Manufactured News." In: *The Manufacture of News: Social Problems, Deviance and the Mass Media*, edited by Stanley Cohen and Jock Young. London: Constable. Pp. 226–241.

Coleman, James S. (1974). *Power and the Structure of Society*. New York: Norton.

Ditton, Jason and James Duffy (1983). "Bias in the Newspaper Reporting of Crime News." *British Journal of Criminology* 23 (April):159–165.

Dussuyer, I. (1978). "Crime News: A Study of 40 Ontario Newspapers." Toronto, Canada: Center of Criminology, University of Toronto.

Ermann, M. David and Richard L. Lundman (1978). *Corporate and Governmental Deviance: Problems of Organizational Behavior in Contemporary Society*. New York: Oxford University Press.

Evans, Sandra S. and Richard L. Lundman (1983). "Newspaper Coverage of Corporate Price-Fixing." *Criminology* 21 (November):529–541.

Fellmeth, Robert C. (1970). *The Interstate Commerce Omission: The Public Interest and the ICC*. New York: Grossman.

Fishman, Mark (1978). "Crime Waves as Ideology." *Social Problems* 25 (June):531–543.

Galliher, James R. and James A. Cain (1974). "Citation Support for the Mafia Myth in Criminology Textbooks." *American Sociologist* 9 (May):68–74.

Garofalo, James (1981). "Crime and the Mass Media: A Selective Review of Research." *Journal of Research in Crime and Delinquency* 18 (July):319–350.

Graber, Doris Appel (1980). *Crime News and the Public*. New York: Praeger.

Hall, Stuart, Charles Critcher, Tony Jefferson, John Clark, and Brian Roberts (1978). *Policing the Crisis: Mugging, the State, and Law and Order*. London: MacMillan Press.

McCann, Eamonn (1973). "The British Press and Northern Ireland." In: *The Manufacture of News: Social Problems, Deviance and the*

*Mass Media*, edited by Stanley Cohen and Jock Young. London: Constable. Pp. 242–261.

Molotch, Harvey and Marilyn Lester (1975). "Accidental News: The Great Oil Spill as Local Occurrence and National Event." *American Journal of Sociology* 81 (September):235–260.

Murdock, Graham (1973). "Political Deviance: The Press Presentation of a Militant Mass Demonstration." In: *The Manufacture of News: Social Problems, Deviance and the Mass Media.* edited by Stanley Cohen and Jock Young. London: Constable. Pp. 156–175.

Quinney, Richard (1979). *Criminology.* Boston: Little Brown.

Reiss, Albert (1983). "The Policing of Organizational Life." In: *Control in the Police Organization*, edited by Maurice Punch. Cambridge, MA: MIT Press. Pp. 78–97.

Rock, Paul (1973). "News as External Recurrence." In: *The Manufacture of News: Social Problems, Deviance and the Mass Media*, edited by Stanley Cohen and Jock Young. London: Constable. Pp. 73–80.

Roshier, Rob (1973). "The Selection of Crime News by the Press." In: *The Manufacture of News: Social Problems, Deviance and the Mass Media*, edited by Stanley Cohen and Jock Young. London: Constable. Pp. 28–39.

Sherizen, Sanford (1978). "Social Creation of Crime News: All the News Fitted to Print." In: *Deviance and Mass Media*, edited by Charles Winick. Beverly Hills: Sage. Pp. 203–224.

Sutherland, Edwin H. (1949). *White collar Crime.* New York: Holt, Rinehart and Winston.

U.S. Senate (1978). *Hearings Before the Subcommittee on Antitrust Monopoly of the Committee on the Judiciary on Competition in the Trucking Industry.* 95th Congress. 2nd Session.